KISMET

KISMET

(A Musical Arabian Night)

Music and Lyrics by

ROBERT WRIGHT *and* GEORGE FORREST

(*from the themes of* ALEXANDER BORODIN)

Book by

CHARLES LEDERER *and* LUTHER DAVIS

(*based on the play by* EDWARD KNOBLOCK)

FRANK MUSIC CO. LTD.,

MADE IN ENGLAND

KISMET

The Edwin Lester production of KISMET *was first presented by Charles Lederer at the Ziegfeld Theatre, New York City, on December 3, 1953, the first London performance was at the Stoll Theatre on April 20, 1955.*

CHARACTERS

IMAM OF THE MOSQUE	SECOND POLICEMAN
MUEZZINS	THE WAZIR OF POLICE
DOORMAN	WAZIR'S GUARDS
FIRST BEGGAR	LALUME
SECOND BEGGAR	ATTENDANTS
THIRD BEGGAR	THE PRINCESSES OF ABABU
DERVISHES	THE CALIPH
OMAR	SLAVE GIRLS
A PUBLIC POET, LATER CALLED HAJJ	A PEDDLER
MARSINAH, HIS DAUGHTER	A SERVANT
A MERCHANT	PRINCESS ZUBBEDIYA OF DAMASCUS
HASSAN-BEN	AYAH TO ZUBBEDIYA
JAWAN	PRINCESS SAMARIS OF BANGALORE
STREET DANCER	AYAH TO SAMARIS
AKBAR	STREET WOMEN
ASSIZ	PROSECUTOR
THE BANGLE MAN	THE WIDOW YUSSEF
CHIEF POLICEMAN	DIWAN DANCERS

Dancers and Singers

SYNOPSIS OF SCENES
ONE DAY IN BAGHDAD

ACT I
(From Dawn to Dusk)

Scene 1. On the steps of the Mosque.
Scene 2. A tent just outside the city.
Scene 3. The Bazaar of the Caravans.
Scene 4. A side street.
Scene 5. A garden.
Scene 6. A street near the Bazaar.
Scene 7. The throne room of His Exalted Excellency, The Wazir of Police.

ACT II
(From Dusk to Dawn)

Scene 1. Along the route of the Caliph's procession.
Scene 2. The garden.
Scene 3. Anteroom to the Wazir's harem.
Scene 4. A rooftop pavilion in the Wazir's Palace.
Scene 5. A corridor in the Wazir's Palace.
Scene 6. Anteroom to the Wazir's harem.
Scene 7. The ceremonial hall of the Caliph's Palace.

MUSICAL CONTENTS

ACT I

ACT II

SCENE 1

MUSIC No. I—OVERTURE

Outside a mosque in ancient Baghdad; dawn.
As the curtain rises the stage is in shadows and the world
is very quiet. An old man, the IMAM *of this mosque, is*
the only soul awake—he walks slowly across toward the
mosque carrying a lantern and looking up toward the
fading stars.

MUSIC No. I (contd.)—" SANDS OF TIME "

IMAM [*Singing softly to himself*].

Princes come, Princes go,
An hour of pomp and show they know;
Princes come,
And over the sands,
And over the sands of time,
They go!

Wise men come,
Ever promising
The riddle of life to know;
Wise men come,
Ah, but over the sands,
The silent sands of time,
They go!

Lovers come, lovers go,
And all that there is to know
Lovers know,
Only lovers know!

He opens the door of the mosque and steps in as, quite
suddenly, the shrill, carrying voices of muezzins begin to
call the faithful to prayer. The muezzins shriek their
cries from the minarets of the city, their chants actually
issuing from the rear of the theatre, the balcony, and
backstage.

FIRST MUEZZIN	SECOND MUEZZIN	THIRD MUEZZIN	FOURTH MUEZZIN
Allah is mighty			
Mohamed is			
His prophet	Pray'r is bet-		
Pray ye!	ter than sleep		
Pray ye	Pray ye!	Allah	
well!	Pray ye	is a-	
Sleep not com-	well!	wake:	Thy God
placent	Pray ye!	Wake ye	inclines
While thy soul		and pray!	His ear!
Shrivels Shrivels			
Pray, pray!			

Wakened by these Oriental alarm clocks, three ragged
beggars raise their heads from beds of rags in front of the
mosque; they yawn and stretch.
As the voices of the muezzins begin to die away, the FIRST
BEGGAR *gets to his feet and makes a resentful gesture*
toward the nearest minaret.

FIRST BEGGAR [*Spoken resignedly*]. **Every morning that same horrible**
noise! [*He wags his head at his fellows.*] **What an hour to start working.**
I swear, sometimes I wish I wasn't a beggar. [*Nudging* SECOND BEGGAR
roughly with his foot.] **Get up! Get up, and start suffering.** [*He sees a group of*
early morning worshippers approaching, and quickly warns his companions.]

Customers! Hurry ...

Hastily assuming their professional postures, the beggars whine for alms. The worshippers reward them with a few coins before disappearing into the mosque.

BEGGARS [*Spoken*].   Alms! Alms for the love of Allah!   It is written that he who gives gains merit in heaven ... Alms! Alms! Gain virtue by giving.

As the beggars are about to relax and count their earnings, OMAR *enters. He is an old reprobate of talent and wisdom. The beggars crowd around him.*

Alms for the love of Allah! Oh high and mighty—give to the poor. Alms!

OMAR [*Spoken automatically, as he brushes the beggars aside*].   May Allah give thee ease, may Allah give thee ease ...

He finds his way barred by the THIRD BEGGAR *who, being a dervish, is whirling eagerly.* OMAR *glares at him.*

Oh, stop it! [*Music stops.*]

The dervish subsides. OMAR *continues toward the mosque and extends a coin toward the top step, obviously expecting a beggar to take it. There is no beggar there.* OMAR *stops in surprise and blinks at the vacant step.*

What's this? Where is old Hajj?

FIRST BEGGAR.   Gone to make the Holy Pilgrimage, Great Omar.

OMAR.   Off to Mecca? At his age?

FIRST BEGGAR [*Thrusting out his palm*].   Even so. And with Hajj gone, I'm senior beggar here.

OMAR [*Petulantly withholding the money*].   All my life I've started the day by giving one dinar to Hajj the Beggar—no, I'm too old to change beggars.

He turns abruptly and vanishes into the mosque. The voice of a PUBLIC POET *hawking his wares is heard in the distance.*

THE POET'S VOICE [*Off stage*].   Rhymes! Fine rhymes ...

FIRST BEGGAR.   Someone comes! [*He starts to lead his fellows in that direction and then stops disgustedly.*]   Never mind! Save your strength!

SECOND BEGGAR.   Why? Who is it?

THE POET.   Rhymes! Fine rhymes ...

FIRST BEGGAR.   Can't you hear? A public poet—probably as penniless as we look. Hide your money.

THE POET enters. He is dressed in clothes that pretend to rather a lot but are badly in need of repair. He has a jaunty but desperate air—the aspect of a man whom hunger has kept young.

THE POET [*Singing*].   Rhymes, fine rhymes, sweet rhymes have I. [*He bows low and speaks.*]   Salaam, noble gentlemen. Any rhymes today?

SECOND BEGGAR.   Be reasonable, man. What use have beggars for rhymes?

THE POET.   Exactly what I came to discuss! More than any other tradesman, does a beggar have need of verses. A catchy jingle with a note of pain ... a pathetic phrase to coax the stubbornest coin. I guarantee you results, gentlemen. Buy one of my poems and I'll return the fee if my verse does not augment your income.

SECOND BEGGAR.   Oh, go away! It's too early in the day to listen to public poets.

THE POET [*Extemporising instantly*].

Too early to eat,
Too early to bed,
Too early to die,
Too early to wed.
All this I grant you,
Of Beggars the king—
But never, oh never
Too early to sing! [*He bows*].

MUSIC No. 2—"RHYMES HAVE I"

Only five dina for that lovely lyrical thought.

He looks hopefully at the beggars, one of whom betrays a flicker of interest. THE POET *sings.*

Rhymes,
Fine rhymes,
Sweet rhymes have I!
Sly rhymes,
Wry rhymes,
Neat rhymes have I!

To a world too prone to be prosaic
I bring my own panacea:
An iota of iambic and a tittle of trochaic
Added to a small amount of onomatopoeia!

Lays
That sing
With rhymes have I!
Couplets (coo-plays)
That ring
Like chimes have I!

Happy rhymes [*Spoken*] like
" Money makes you sunny."
[*Sung*] Spicy rhymes [*Spoken*] like
" Virtue can hurt you."
[*Sung*] Learned rhymes—
[*Spoken*] " The camel's a mammal."
[*Sung*] And others very various
On matters multifarious
[*Spoken*] Like " beard—sheared!"
" Burnoose—loose!"
" Stairs—prayers!"
" Mosque—kiosk!"
[*Sung*] " Minaret and parapet "
And many more that I'll beget betimes,
Rhymes have I! Rhymes have I!
I have

[*Speaking*]
rhymes to suit everyone's particular needs, gentlemen—including yours.

SECOND BEGGAR.   Something like that might be useful.

THE POET.   What an intelligent fellow! Just a moment, friend—my daughter will write one down for you. [*Calls off.*] Marsinah! Marsinah, we are about to make a sale! Marsinah—breakfast!

MARSINAH runs in. She is barefooted, ragged, lovely, and looks even hungrier than her father.

MARSINAH.   A sale, Father? A sale? Where? To whom?

THE POET.   To this diamond in the rough, this modest lover of beauty. Write, Daughter, in large, illuminated letters.

MARSINAH.   Right away! In my very best hand!

THE POET.   Only three dinar—an excellent bargain. [*He begins to compose.*] " The given coin's a living prayer . . . "

SECOND BEGGAR.   Three dinar—No, a beggar can't afford that kind of money.

He moves away. Defeated, THE POET and MARSINAH turn to leave, but two citizens emerge from the mosque and THE POET springs toward these new prospects.

THE POET.   Noble gentlemen whose eyes have been turned toward heaven—a rhyme to bring them back to earth? Choose your topic: Weddings? Birthdays? Openings of Small Businesses? — Love Eternal, Women's Wiles, Glory, Infamy?

[He sings]
Songs of sense
And pertinence
In reference
To all events
And climes,
Rhymes have I !   Rhymes have I !
I have—

He breaks off as the two men turn away and start out
MARSINAH starts to sing. They pause and turn back
to listen.

MARSINAH.   **Rhymes,**
                       Fine rhymes,
                       True rhymes has he !
                       Rhymes,
                       Bright rhymes,
                       New rhymes has he !
                       Thoughtful rhymes—
THE POET *[Joining her]*
          [Spoken] **Like " Learning leads to earning."**
MARSINAH *[Sung]* **Truthful rhymes—**
THE POET *[Spoken]* **" Drinking stops your thinking."**
MARSINAH *[Sung]* **Healthful rhymes—**
THE POET *[Spoken]* **" Sinning is thinning."**
BOTH   *[Sung]* **And others miscellaneous**
                   On matters more extraneous
MARSINAH *[Spoken]* **Like " crutch—**
THE POET *[Spoken]* **Clutch ! "**
MARSINAH   **" Look—**
THE POET   **Hook ! "**
MARSINAH   **" Vagrant—**
THE POET   **Fragrant ! "**
MARSINAH   **" Dervish—**
THE POET   **Curvish ! "**
MARSINAH   **" Horn—**
THE POET   **Warn ! "**
MARSINAH   **" Caravan—**
THE POET   **Afghanistan ! "**
MARSINAH   **" Dromedary—**
THE POET   **Very hairy ! "**
MARSINAH *[Startled]* **Very hairy ?**
THE POET   **Very sorry !**
BOTH   *[Sung]* **Songs of sense**
                   And pertinence
                   In reference
                   To all events
                   And climes,
THE POET   **Rhymes have I,**
MARSINAH   **Rhymes have I,**
THE POET   **Rhymes has she,**
MARSINAH   **Rhymes has he,**
BOTH   **Rhymes have we !   Rhymes have we !**
                   We have rhymes !

Their song finished, they gaze hopefully at the prospective
customers, but their only reward is a backward glance of
amusement as the two citizens walk off.

THE POET *[Bitterly]*. **A man can sell anything in the world except**
poems. Poisons, emetics, false noses—but no poems ! *[To MARSINAH].*
Has your hunger grown ?
MARSINAH *[Trying to chuckle]*. **Like a magic tree.**
THE POET *[Drawing her aside; lowering his voice]*. **The orange market**
will open at any moment.
MARSINAH *[Also lowering her voice]*. **I'll be on time, Father.**

THE POET. **Do not take so many that they interfere with your speed of foot.**

MARSINAH. **My father's wisdom always guides me—When you borrow property, never overburden yourself.** [*She laughs and runs off*].

THE POET [*To himself, as he stares after her*]. **A father who sends his daughter to steal! Could anything be baser than that? Take note, Allah, how low a human can sink—to the bottom!**

Disconsolate, he wanders toward the steps of the mosque where he sinks into a sitting position, too depressed to notice several townspeople approaching the mosque, pursued, as usual, by the beggars. The last of the townspeople, mistaking THE POET *for a beggar, drops a coin into his lap.* THE POET *looks up in surprise, and calls after the donor with a fervour that offers an attractive contrast to the professional gratitude of the beggars.*

Friend, I thank you!

The three beggars stiffen. They approach THE POET *with deliberate menace.*

FIRST BEGGAR. **What are you doing there?**

THE POET. **Sitting. Just sitting.**

SECOND BEGGAR. **But you're not a beggar!**

THE POET. **You don't need to be snobbish about it.**

SECOND BEGGAR. **You can't beg in that spot! That's the best begging location in Baghdad!**

THE POET. **Oh?**

FIRST BEGGAR. **Why do you think it's empty?**

THE POET. **It's not empty. I'm here.**

FIRST BEGGAR. **It must remain empty until old Hajj returns from Mecca!**

SECOND BEGGAR. **It's against the law for anyone not of the Hajj family to beg on the steps of the mosque.**

FIRST BEGGAR. **Get out before we inform the Wazir's police.**

THIRD BEGGAR [*Displaying a hook which he wears in lieu of a right hand*]. **And here's the least that happens to anyone taken by the Wazir's police!**

THE POET *looks from one to the other, swallows deeply and puts on his most urbane smile.*

THE POET [*With all the conviction he can muster*]. **My dear verminous friends, I am a cousin to Hajj. Come, come, consider—only a Hajj may sit here. That is the law. So would I dare risk it if I were not a Hajj? Only a very desperate man would do that.**

SECOND BEGGAR [*Suspiciously*]. **The old man never spoke of relatives.**

THE POET. **Noble beggars, how many of you have relatives of whom you're ashamed?**

As the logic of this observation gives the beggars pause, OMAR *comes out of the mosque, having completed his morning's worship. He stops short, surprised at seeing Hajj's place now occupied.*

BEGGARS [*Ad lib.*]
**That's true—that's true . . .
Absolutely true . . .
Yes, of course . . .
I'd never admit my brother was my brother . . .
Nor me . . .**

OMAR [*To the* POET'S *back*]. **I thought you'd gone to Mecca . . .** [*He breaks off, realizing that this is a stranger. To the* BEGGARS] **Who is this?**

FIRST BEGGAR. **He claims the name of Hajj.**

THE POET [*To* OMAR]. **A customer of Hajj's, I presume?** [*He extends his palm, beggar-fashion*]. **I am taking over his practice.**

OMAR. **I said it before and I'll say it again. I'm too old to change beggars.**

THE POET [*Extemporizing a verse*]
　　　　**You say you're too old to change beggars?
　　　　Your attitude strikes me as strange.**

It's easy enough to change beggars—
What's difficult is, to beg change.

OMAR [*Laughing*].   Not bad, not bad.   [*Taking out a coin*].   You deserve
encouragement.   Here.

> THE POET *is about to accept it but stops when he sees the
> full coin purse from which it came.   He shakes his head*

THE POET.   One dinar is not enough to encourage me.
FIRST BEGGAR [*Deeply shocked*].   Take it, take it!
THE POET.   No, it's too little.   [*To* OMAR]   You're too stingy.   No.
OMAR.   Now the beggars tell us what to give!   [*He sighs in wonderment
at modern ways, but produces an extra coin*].   Here.   But not for the beggar—
for the poet.

> OMAR *exits and* THE POET, *happily rattling the coins in
> his hand, calls after him.*

THE POET.   I thank you!

> *The beggars close in on him again.*

THIRD BEGGAR.   You'll disgrace us!
SECOND BEGGAR.   We mustn't seem to be greedy.   We're not even
supposed to *notice* the amount!
FIRST BEGGAR.   It's the spirit behind the gift that counts!
THE POET.   Never have I seen a profession more keenly in need of
ew blood!

> *A businessman enters, carrying a jug of olives on his
> shoulder.   He pushes rudely past the clamouring beggars
> and starts up the mosque steps.* THE POET *grabs him by
> the coat as he passes.*

THE POET [*Smoothly*].   Give me a few dozen dinar, friend, and an
already pleasant morning will be made pleasanter for both of us.

> *The businessman pulls away indignantly, and raps on
> the mosque door to summon the* IMAM.

If you do not want my blessing I'll be happy to give you my curse.
BUSINESSMAN [*Curtly*].   I don't give money away.   I'm a man of
business.
THE POET.   May the graves of your ancestors vanish in the spring
floods.   [*No reaction from the businessman who knocks again*].   May your
wives betray you with every chimneysweep in Baghdad!   [*Unperturbed,
the businessman raps once more*].   May your sons and daughters defile your
memory!   [*This doesn't work either.* THE POET *considers for a moment*].   May
your taxes increase!

> *The businessman abandons his knocking and hurriedly
> produces a coin; he puts jug down outside mosque door
> and hastily exits as* THE POET *pockets his earnings.*

THE POET.   A beautiful profession, perfectly suited to my talents.
FIRST BEGGAR [*Dumbfounded*].   I never saw a beggar curse a man into
giving!
THE POET.   This business is under new management!

> *Worshippers come out of the mosque and the beggars pur-
> sue them.   Instead of their former cry of "Alms for the
> love of Allah," they shout "May your taxes increase."
> Their new technique produces instant profits.   They
> huddle together, excitedly comparing their gains.* THE
> POET, *alone on the steps for the moment, rattles his new
> wealth in his hand, and feels moved to compose a verse:*

THE POET.   Three dinar, three whole dinar and all because I an-
swered when opportunity summoned.
                    [*Spoken*]
THE POET   I sat down, feeling desolated,
                  Bowed my head and crossed my knees—
                  Is fortune really predicated
                  Upon such tiny turns as these?

MUSIC No. 3—"FATE"

[*Spoken*]
Then Fate's a thing without a head,
A puzzle never understood,
And man proceeds where he is led,
Unguaranteed of bad or good.
[*Sings*]
Fate! Fate can be the trap in your path,
The bitter cup of your tears,
Your wine of wrath!
Fate can be shade in the desert blaze,
Sudden food in a famine found,
The sound of praise!

Incomprehensible and strange,
Fate can play a trick with the twine
To weave the evil and good
In one design!

And so, my Destiny,
I look at you and cannot see—
Is it good, is it ill?
Am I blessed, am I cursed?
Is it honey on my tongue or brine?
What fate, what fate is mine?

Fate can play a trick with the twine
To weave the evil and good
In one design!

And so, my Destiny,
I look at you and cannot see—
Is it good, is it ill?
Am I blessed, am I cursed?
Is it honey on my tongue or brine?
What fate, what fate is—

He breaks off as three giant brigands appear stage L. *The leader,* HASSAN-BEN, *is of ferocious mien; the other two are enormous, half-naked men wearing many weapons. Their appearance causes the beggars to shrink back in terror.* HASSAN-BEN *brutally shoves the dervish out of his way, sending him sprawling, and then stabs a forefinger in the direction of* THE POET. *Music continues under dialogue.*

HASSAN-BEN. You on the steps—come here!
THE POET [*Affably*]. Good morning, Oh, Giant Man of the Desert . . . Welcome to civilization.

Hopefully he extends his hand for alms. A cold glare is his reply. THE POET *hesitates. Then he recovers his courage and advances toward* HASSAN-BEN.

HASSAN-BEN. Are you the beggar called Hajj?
THE POET [*He starts to deny it, then remembers his impersonation*]. Even so am I. Far and wide the name of Hajj is . . . [*The desert trio whip out their gleaming scimitars.* THE POET *tries to retreat*]. Permit me to correct myself, my name is *not* Hajj . . . [*But the brigands, disbelieving this sudden denial, halt him by rapping on the ground with their swords;* HASSAN-BEN *thrusts a knife toward* THE POET's *ribs, holding him at bay*]. Gentlemen, you are making a mistake! Who are you, what do you want? . . . [*They throw him to the ground and seize him by the legs*]. I know what you are! You're slavers! Slavers! Allaaaaaaaah!

His yells of protest fade into the distance as the brigands drag him away. The music of "Fate" rises as the lights dim.

MUSIC No. 4—"THE HAND OF FATE" (change of Scene)

SCENE 2

The interior of an elaborate tent just outside the walls of Baghdad. JAWAN, *a very old, infirm, and myopic master brigand, is pacing impatiently. He carries a heavy whip, and brims with suppressed violence. A small charcoal brazier glows from a tripod at one side of the tent.*
HASSAN-BEN *strides in.*

HASSAN-BEN [*Triumphant*]. **Master, Hajj the Beggar!**
JAWAN [*Smiling at the red brazier*]. **Good. The fire is ready.**

THE POET *is hauled in, still protesting.*

THE POET. **. . . but such a profitless error—a mere beggar! I have nothing. My pockets are empty!** [*Seeing* JAWAN]. **Oh, glorious chieftain, let me be, I pray you! I'm not worth selling at the slave market. Look, my bad leg, injured in a fall, unable to bear my weight. I am old, foolish, forgetful and broken-brained . . . I am worthless. Less than worthless!**
JAWAN [*To* HASSAN-BEN]. **Talks a lot, doesn't he?** [*Leaning down toward* THE POET]. **You know me?**
THE POET [*Hysterically*]. **I know no one—and nothing. I have no memory.**
JAWAN. **I am Jawan.**
THE POET [*In horror*]. **Jawan!! Oh, no!**
JAWAN. **Ah, your memory freshens.**
THE POET [*Prattling with fear*]. **Well, it's a famous name . . . Jawan? . . .** **It strikes a chord. Let me see, you're Jawan, yes, the great astronomer.**
JAWAN [*Striking out with his whip*]. **You dissemble poorly. I am Jawan, the Robber, the Brigand—as you very well know.**
THE POET. **But I** *don't* **know. I have no interest in such matters. By tomorrow I will have forgotten your face.** [*Hopefully*]. **I could never identify you.**
JAWAN [*To the brigands*]. **Tie him down and bare his belly.**
THE POET [*His voice rising*]. **Why? What for?**
JAWAN. **We are going to decorate it with a red hot coal sparkling in its navel, like a jewel.**
THE POET. **Why? In Allah's name, what have I done?**
JAWAN *To* HASSAN-BEN]. **Can it be he has forgotten?** [*To* THE POET]. **Recall you [the curse you put upon me fifteen years ago, Hajj the Beggar?**
THE POET [*Desperately*]. **Believe me, I have only been Hajj the Beggar since this morning!**
JAWAN [*To* HASSAN-BEN]. **His mind has rotted. Like a fig.**

He is mysteriously pleased at this notion.

THE POET. **I swear to you! I have never seen you before!**
JAWAN. **I know that—but fifteen years ago you put a curse upon my name.** [*He advances threateningly*]. **And soon after that my only son was stolen from me! All these years I have sought my son. Everywhere. I have offered ransom that would purchase all of Persia. None came to claim it. And now, I shall die soon.**
THE POET [*With a great show of sympathy*]. **Oh, let's hope not!**
JAWAN. **I must find my son in the few weeks remaining to me. The wise men tell me it is your curse that keeps me from him.**
THE POET [*A sudden calm coming over him*]. **Do they really? And how much ransom did you say you offered?**
JAWAN [*Fiercely*]. **Never mind the ransom! Remove the curse!**
THE POET. **Of course. Certainly. Delighted to do the best I can— under these conditions.**
JAWAN. **Don't haggle with me! Remove the curse!**

14

THE POET. **Mighty Jawan, you don't understand. A curse must be removed voluntarily. That is the law of curses. After all, a curse is nothing but a prayer, a prayer for harm. And a prayer is born in the heart, Jawan, not in the mouth!**

JAWAN [*Impressed with this reasoning*]. **And you'd not pray for me and mean it.**

THE POET [*Quickly*]. **For money I would!**

JAWAN. **Ass! Would Allah heed a prayer that's paid for?**

THE POET. **Aye! Indeed so. Do you not give money to mosques, and to holy men? And do they not bless you and pray for you?**

JAWAN [*Excited*]. **That is true! True!** [*To* HASSAN-BEN]. **Give him a gold piece.**

THE POET [*Snatching the gold piece*]. **Is this all your son is worth to you?**

JAWAN [*Ominously*]. **If my patience snaps . . .**

THE POET. **. . . You'll have eternity to regret it. Think, Jawan! Listen to death chuckling in your chest! What good will your wealth be when the chuckle becomes a roar? Do I not offer you your son, happiness on earth—as well as a cushion in Paradise? How much is too much for eternal bliss?**

JAWAN. **You tongue is cunning. Take ten gold pieces.**

THE POET. **A hundred!**

JAWAN [*Startled*]. **A hun—!** [*He stops and considers a moment*]. **Will I find my son this day?**

THE POET. **Possibly within the hour!**

> JAWAN *regards him piercingly for a moment. Then he gestures to* HASSAN-BEN *who obediently produces a heavy purse. He is about to hand this to* THE POET *when he sees that* JAWAN *is putting on his cloak, clearly intending to leave.*

HASSAN-BEN [*Alarmed*]. **Master! Don't risk entering the city! You'll be taken by the Wazir's police! Tortured, beheaded!**

JAWAN. **If it is written that I am to die in Baghdad, how shall I avoid it?**

HASSAN-BEN [*Simply*]. **By staying** *out* **of Baghdad.**

JAWAN. **No man may avoid his fate. That is Kismet.**

> *He gestures commandingly and* HASSAN-BEN *throws the purse at* THE POET'S *feet.*

THE POET [*Eyeing the purse*]. **I thank you. Now, leave me to my prayers.** [*He starts to kneel, but then suddenly pauses and asks, a trifle apologetically*]. **Excuse me, which way** *is* **Mecca?**

> *In unison the brigands point out the correct direction and* THE POET *kneels. His fingers inch toward the purse on the ground beside him as he pretends to concentrate on his prayers. Satisfied with his bona fides, the others turn away, preparing to depart.*

MUSIC No. 5—" FATE "—REPRISE

JAWAN [*Spoken*]. **Farewell.**

> *He goes out.* HASSAN-BEN *the last to leave, glares at* THE POET.

HASSAN-BEN [*Spoken*]. **Pray well, Hajj the Beggar!**

> *He exits;* THE POET *looks around to make sure he's alone. Then he seizes the purse and clutches it to him.*

THE POET [*Spoken*]. **I'm rich!** *I* **am rich! On the rim of torture and death—and now treasure. Why, I'm the richest man I ever knew!**

> *He kisses the purse and begins to sing.*

>> **Today's my day—**
>> **My day of days!**
>> **My blessings unfold**
>> **In a hundred golden ways!**

Fate has played the trick with the twine
And woven evil and good in one design!
And I can face the sun—
No more to dodge, no more to run!
I can eat, I can buy,
I can sleep in a bed
In the certainty I'm fed and free!
For fate has claimed its child
And smiled
On me!

*He races out. The lights black out and the music of
"Bazaar of the Caravans" is heard.*

ACT I SCENE 3

SCENE 3

MUSIC No. 6—" BAZAAR OF THE CARAVANS "

The Bazaar of the Caravans, just inside the gates of the city. Tradesmen of every description—purveyors of panaceas, pearls, or people—cry their wares in song as they stroll through the hive of shoppers. Near one of the hawkers' booths gay alley-dwellers make a splash of colour and movement as they twirl in the pattern of a street dance.

A trumpet fanfare sounds in the distance, and the Bazaar of the Caravans abruptly becomes silent. All motion stops and all smiles cease as an approaching voice roars "Make way! Make way for the Wazir of Police!" The citizens exchange apprehensive glances and sink to their knees. A squad of black-garbed WAZIR'S *police march in*

BANGLE MEN AND MERCHANTS
Baubles, bangles and Beads,
Buy, oh noble buyer,
Buy your merchandise from us!
These wares are supreme!
Baubles, bangles and beads!
Baubles, bangles and beads!

TOWNSWOMEN
Marvellous!
Marvellous!
Unbelievable!
Thrilling!

VENDOR AND SHOPPER
All the way from Egypt
By camel and by sail.
None other can compare.

TOWNSWOMEN
How fair, how rare!

VENDORS
Buy, oh noble buyer, buy!
And buy, and buy and buy and
buy and buy!

SHOPPERS
Oh, with such a lot to buy,
The busy buyer is lost!
To make up his mind
A problem.
Which are the best goods?
Are there other goods better?

TWO SILK MERCHANTS
We handle silk of China,
No finer silken robes.

PEARL MERCHANT
Pearls, pearls,
Girls' pearls!

WAZIR'S POLICEMAN. **Bow low! The Wazir comes! The mighty Wazir of Police who has eyes everywhere!**

A BRAVE MERCHANT [*From safety in the rear*]. **Except in his wife's bedroom!**

This rebellious jape elicits some merriment from the kneeling townspeople. The echo of their laughter still hangs in the air as the WAZIR OF POLICE *enters. He is a porcine young man, black-browed and petulant. His platoon of escorts bristles with weapons. The sound of people laughing has caused the* WAZIR *to frown.*

WAZIR [*To his* CHIEF POLICEMAN]. **Investigate that laughter. If their merriment relates to me, see how well they laugh without teeth.**

CHIEF POLICEMAN. **It shall be done, Oh, Wazir.**

The teeth of a goodly segment of the population of Baghdad are saved by a sudden shout from the direction of the great city gates.

HERALD'S VOICE. **Wife of Wives to the Wazir! Wife of Wives to the Wazir! Persons of ordinary rank, clear the Bazaar!**

MUSIC No. 7—ENTRANCE OF LALUME

The policemen move to enforce the herald's request. No one showing an inclination to loiter, the Bazaar is quickly cleared.

A closed litter borne by half-naked slave men is carried in and deposited near the WAZIR. *Its curtains part to reveal the voluptuous and restless young creature who is the* WAZIR'S *Wife of Wives. She is clothed in silk and scented oil, and her name is* LALUME.

18

LALUME. **Salaam, my exalted husband.**

WAZIR [*Kissing her hand*]. **Salaam, Lalume, possessor of my entire heart. Happiness attends your return.**

LALUME [*Glancing about as she steps out of the litter*]. **That's a new guard, isn't it? That tall one?**

WAZIR. **Never mind the new guard! I sent you to Ababu to negotiate a loan. Did you get it or not?**

LALUME. **Do you really wish to discuss your private business in a public square?**

WAZIR. [*Furiously*]. **Lalume, without that loan, I perish! Answer me! Do I get it?**

LALUME. **Untrouble your face, My Lord. You do . . . All the gold ten camels can carry.**

WAZIR [*Delighted*]. **Splendid! Splendid!**

LALUME. **But the condition is a high marriage for the three princesses of Ababu.**

WAZIR. **I don't want any more wives! You know very well, I don't even use all the ones I've got.**

LALUME. **My Lord, no one knows that better than I. But it is not you the Shiek of Ababu wishes his daughters to marry.**

WAZIR. **Who, then?**

LALUME. **The Commander of the Faithful, our noble Caliph himself.**

WAZIR. **Well, that should not be too difficult to arrange. The Caliph has no Wife of Wives. Are these Ababus attractive?**

LALUME. **You shall see for yourself, my Lord.** [*She claps her hands, summoning her slaves who bring an enormous, covered wicker basket*]. **Assume your gentlest manner—the Princesses are already homesick and as shy as a little herd of deer. Exalted Wazir, may I present their Royal Highnesses, the Princesses of Ababu?**

MUSIC No. 8—ABABU DANCE I

The wicker basket opens and from it erupt three tiny Asiatic maidens. They are young and pretty, and astonishingly warlike. Each brandishes a sword and buckler. They perform a brief, violent dance which presumably is a common ceremony of greeting in the mountain fastnesses of Ababu. Startled, the WAZIR *backs away from the flailing swords that threaten to behead him. Abruptly* THE PRINCESSES *end their salutation by falling prone before him. The* WAZIR *takes a deep breath in relief*

LALUME. **Princesses of Ababu, allow me—my exalted husband, the Wazir of Baghdad.**

FIRST PRINCESS. **I am honoured.**

SECOND PRINCESS. **And I.**

THIRD PRINCESS. **And I.**

WAZIR. **In the name of our illustrious Caliph, I welcome you to Baghdad.**

He steps forward to greet them more personally but they alert their swords, probably defending themselves against some imagined assault on their persons. They confer in their own language:

FIRST PRINCESS. **Baghdad arakazoots.**

SECOND PRINCESS. **Set sen!**

THIRD PRINCESS. **Set sen!**

WAZIR [*Nervously to his* CHIEF POLICEMAN]. **What did they say?**

CHIEF POLICEMAN [*Interpreting unwillingly*]. **They say they could not be happy here, no matter what their father wants.**

WAZIR [*Offended*]. **Not happy in Baghdad? That's impossible!**

LALUME [*Amused*]. **Unthinkable!**

WAZIR. **Why, Baghdad is the symbol of happiness on earth!** [*Aside* CHIEF POLICEMAN]. **Go fetch me fifty happy people— quickly!**

CHIEF POLICEMAN. **My Lord, it would take me a month!**

WAZIR.   **Then scatter some coins in the street.   Hurry!**

The policemen rush upstage where they sow the street with coins. Attracted by the tinkling of currency, a bevy of townspeople instantly gathers. The WAZIR *smiles encouragingly at* THE PRINCESSES.

Those who live in Baghdad fear only that they may be deafened by the ceaseless cries of merriment, of joy, and of pleasure!

He points triumphantly to where people are gathering up the coins with many shrill cries of delight and astonishment.

See them!   The entire populace laughing and dancing from morning till night!

FIRST PRINCESS [*Dubiously to her sisters*].   **Arakazoots espaniya?**

SECOND PRINCESS [*Derogatory in tone*].   **Nyesets!**

THIRD PRINCESS [*To* LALUME].   **We wish to go home.**

The WAZIR *darts an appealing glance at* LALUME *who steps forward to confront* THE PRINCESSES.

LALUME [*Persuasively*].   **But our city is the world's gayest playground! There's been nothing like it for a thousand years!**

MUSIC No. 9—" NOT SINCE NINEVEH "

[*Sings*] **Baghdad!   Don't underestimate Baghdad!**

WAZIR [*Joining in the song*]
A city rich in romantic oriental lore!

TOWNSPEOPLE.   **Aye!**

LALUME.   **Baghdad!   You must investigate Baghdad!**

WAZIR.   **And learn a few of the facts you never knew before!**

TOWNSPEOPLE.   **Aye!**

LALUME.   **Due south of the Garden of Eden,**
Due north of the Gulf of Aden,
Where every male and maiden
Is laden down
With the blisses of Baghdad,
This irresistible town!

When or where
Could you compare
High life
To the life you find here?
Not since Nineveh, not since Tyre,
Not since Babylon turned to mire
For a sin of a kind we never mind here!

Where or when
Ever again
Low life
Like the life well known here?
Not since Nineveh, not since Sidon,
Not since Jericho started slidin'
From the din of a horn that's never blown here!

Our palaces are gaudier,
Our alleyways are bawdier,
Our princes more autocratic here,
Our beggars more distinctly aromatic here!

Where could you
Ever pursue
Your life
With the zeal we feel here?
Not since Babylon read that writing,
Not since Jericho heard that trumpet,
Not since Nebuchadnezzar's hanging garden went
**   to pot,**

Not since that village near Gomorrah got
Too hot
For Lot!
No, not since Nineveh,
Not since Nineveh . . .

Nineveh!

The WAZIR *has busied himself rounding up a crowd of bystanders, who now, in obedience to his gestures, join in the song.* THE PRINCESSES *continue to listen with a noncommittal air.*

TOWNSPEOPLE. Come to Baghdad, live in Baghdad!
Life in Baghdad takes you back to Nineveh!
LALUME AND TOWNSPEOPLE [*Shouting*]
Nineveh!

THE PRINCESSES *decide to consult. They form a tight little huddle and whisper agitatedly. The* WAZIR *sidles toward them and tries to eavesdrop but one of* THE PRINCESSES *pops her head out of the huddle and stares at him menacingly. He smiles weakly and snaps his fingers at the onlookers who take up a rhythmic chant:*

MUSIC No. 10—NOT SINCE NINEVEH—DANCE

TOWNSPEOPLE [*Spoken*]
Stay in Baghdad!
Stay in Baghdad; Stay in Baghdad!

The WAZIR *looks frantically about for reinforcements. His gaze falls upon two bare-chested young swains of the city. He motions them toward* THE PRINCESSES. *Their appearance breaks up the huddle and the young men and* THE PRINCESSES *dance flirtatiously.*

TOWNSPEOPLE [*Singing*]   *During the dance:*
When or where
Could you compare
High life
To the life you find here?
Not since Nineveh, not since Tyre
Not since Babylon turned to mire
For a sin of a kind we never mind here!
Where could you
Ever pursue
Your life
With the zeal we feel here?
Not since Babylon read that writing
Not since Jericho heard that trumpet
Not
Not since
No!
No! No! No, not since Nineveh
Not since
Not since Nineveh, not since Tyre
Not since Babylon turned to mire
Not since Nineveh, not since Sidon,
Not since Jericho started slidin',
Baghdad is the gayest town since Nineveh!
[*Shouted*] Nineveh!

Finally THE THREE PRINCESSES *seem convinced—at least for the moment. Before they have a chance to reconsider, three stalwart policemen take them pick-a-back toward the* WAZIR'S *Palace.*

MUSIC No. 11—EXIT AFTER NINEVEH and STOLEN ORANGES

The WAZIR *and* LALUME *and their retinues follow; the townspeople return to their normal habits of buying and selling; merchants resume crying their wares in song. Suddenly* MARSINAH *runs in clutching some stolen oranges. An* ORANGE MERCHANT *follows in close and raging pursuit. When* MARSINAH *sees that she is going to be caught, she stops, hurls the oranges out of sight, and leans against a vendor's wagon trying to look innocent. The* ORANGE MERCHANT *grabs her by the arm and twists it cruelly.*

ORANGE MERCHANT. **Where are they? Where are they, sticky-fingered street girl? Where are the oranges you stole?**

MARSINAH [*Gasping in pain*]. **I? I took no oranges, I but touched them to feel their freshness. But they were soft and old and smelt bad—like you!**

He gives a cry of rage and strikes her heavily. She falls to the ground as THE POET *appears in the background.*

ORANGE MERCHANT. **You impudent thief! I'll have my oranges back—or kick your bones apart!**

He is about to do so but THE POET *springs forward and knocks the* ORANGE MERCHANT *sprawling.*

THE POET [*His foot pressing the* ORANGE MERCHANT'S *neck*]. **Rest a while, father of none and son of hundreds! Rest till I learn if my daughter be harmed!**

MARSINAH. **No, Father! It's all right. Let him up, let him go away!**

THE POET. **Up then, toad!**

ORANGE MERCHANT [*Scrambling to his feet and retreating*]. **I'll have you jailed for this!** [*He exits, caressing his jaw.*]

MARSINAH. **Come, Father, before he summons the police.**

She tugs at her father's arm. He grins back at her, holding his purse of gold behind his back.

THE POET. **Marsinah, we don't run away from the police. Not any more.**

MARSINAH. **Why not?**

THE POET. **Because of what I hold behind my back!**

MARSINAH. **What is it?**

THE POET [*Exuberantly*]. **It can be anything you've ever wanted—or everything!** [*He rattles the pouch*]. **What does it sound like?**

MARSINAH [*Unable to believe what she hears*]. **Not copper pieces?**

THE POET. **No, not** *copper* **pieces.** [*She looks disappointed and baffled. He tries a new tack*]. **Marsinah, suppose you could have anything in the world you wanted. What would you wish for?**

MARSINAH. **Breakfast!**

THE POET [*Dryly*]. **Imagine you've had your breakfast.**

MARSINAH [*Equally dryly*]. **Tell me how to do that and I'll never ask for anything else.**

THE POET [*Becoming impatient*]. **Daughter, indulge me—speak! Of all the things in the world, what do you wish for most?**

MARSINAH [*Thinking hard*]. **Fresh straw for our corner of the camel stable.**

THE POET [*Pained*]. **Dear child, let us have some breadth of vision! Think big! Very big!**

MARSINAH [*In a burst of imagination*]. **The other half of the blanket! We could buy the other half of the blanket!**

THE POET [*Calling to nearby tradesmen*]. **Good merchants, set forth your silks and jewels, your finest garments, and sweetest perfumes! My daughter will purchase only the best!**

MERCHANT [*As bystanders laugh*]. **Who is this happy madman?**

THE POET [*Pouring gold from the purse into* MARSINAH'S *hand*]. **Those who are slow to serve us will naturally be the last to receive our custom.**

> *The bystanders gasp in amazement. We hear cries of "It's gold! Real gold!" and they crowd closer. However* MARSINAH *immediately suspects the worst. Frightened she leads* THE POET *aside.*

MARSINAH. **Father, Father, put it back where you got it!**
THE POET. **Never fear, child. It is honestly got, honestly got! Here.** [*He pours more coins into her hand*].
MARSINAH. **Father, I'm afraid!**
THE POET. **Sweet Marsinah, our frightened days are behind us!** [*Tenderly*]. **Marsinah, we are rich enough to buy the house and garden—the one you've coveted so long you've forgotten how to wish for it! But don't tell the owner our name. I may need to find myself a new identity until a certain old brigand rejoins his ancestors.**
MARSINAH. **Then it *is* stolen!**
THE POET. **No! Believe me, believe me! Here!** [*He tosses the purse into her lap*].
MARSINAH. **But—keep some of the money for yourself! You talk only of things for me.**
THE POET [*Disdaining the purse*]. **What does a poet need? What can rival the beautiful things he invents in his own head?**

> *As if in answer to this rhetorical question, a slave merchant leads four lovely slave girls across the bazaar, calling "I have girls! Able-bodied slave girls for sale or rent!"* THE POET *stares thoughtfully after the girls as they sway away from him. After a moment of contemplation he turns back to* MARSINAH *and plucks the purse from her lap.*

Come to think of it . . .
MARSINAH [*Straight-faced*]. **Think of what, Father?**
THE POET [*A transparent hypocrite*]. **Well, you should have maids and attendants now. It's only fitting for a young lady in your position.** [*Anxiously*]. **Don't you think so?**
MARSINAH [*Teasing*]. **I wouldn't know what to do with them.**
THE POET. **Oh, I'll find some way to keep them busy.**
MARSINAH. **Whatever you say, Father.**
THE POET. **I'll get three or four. No sense being short-handed.**

> *He hurries out.* MARSINAH *laughs delightedly, feels the money in her hands and turns toward the Bazaar booth. The merchants, who have been waiting their chance, immediately surround her and display their wares.*

MUSIC No. 12—" BAUBLES, BANGLES AND BEADS "

MARSINAH [*Spoken*]. **So many beautiful things! What should I buy?**

> MARSINAH'S *eye is caught by an aged pedlar of bracelets rings and other baubles who wanders the Bazaar:*

BANGLEMAN [*Singing*]
        Baubles, bangles and beads!

> MARSINAH *attempts to follow him but is blocked by eager merchants who thrust their wares at her.*

MERCHANTS.   **Marsinah buy from me!**
                 Marsinah, lovely Marsinah, buy!
SILK MERCHANTS [*Singing*]
        Worms work on a Chinese terrace,
        Worms dream of a happy heiress
        Wearing their wares!
        Answer their prayers! Answer their prayers!
        Buy our silken wares!

> *She is diverted from the silks they dangle before her when the* BANGLEMAN *reiterates his cry:*

BANGLEMAN.   **Baubles, bangles and beads!**

MARSINAH [*Singing as she moves toward him*]
> Baubles, bangles,
> Hear how they jing, jing-a-ling-a,
> Baubles, bangles,
> Bright shiny beads!

Once more the other merchants bar her from the BANGLE-MAN, *urgently voicing their pleas:*

MERCHANTS. **Marsinah buy from me!**
Marsinah, lovely Marsinah, buy!

PEARL MERCHANT [*Singing*]
> Think upon the Macedonian oyster
> Having indigestion in his watery cloister
> So that Marsinah could have a pearl,
> A pearl, a pearl!

BANGLEMAN. **Baubles, bangles and beads!**

She brushes past the merchants and hurries toward the BANGLEMAN. *At this moment two newcomers enter the Bazaar. One is* OMAR, *whom we have met in the first scene. He is accompanied by a handsome, thoughtful young man who is the* CALIPH, *incognito. His gaze falls upon this delightful young girl who is the focus of all eyes in the Bazaar. He stops short and watches as she rapturously examines the* BANGLEMAN'S *stock of trinkets.*

MARSINAH [*Singing*]
> Baubles, bangles,
> Hear how they jing, jing-a-ling-a,
> Baubles, bangles,
> Bright shiny beads,
> Sparkles, spangles,
> My heart will sing, sing-a-ling-a,
> Wearing baubles, bangles and beads.
> I'll glitter and gleam so,
> Make somebody dream so
> That some day he may
> Buy me a ring, ring-a-ling-a,
> I've heard that's where it leads,
> Wearing baubles, bangles and beads.

She drops an earring. The CALIPH *moves forward swiftly and retrieves it.*

CALIPH [*Singing to her as he returns the earring*]
> Often that's where it leads,
> Wearing baubles, bangles and beads!

Their eyes meet. Perhaps the CALIPH *would have spoken but they are interrupted by several young women. Music continues under dialogue.*

FIRST YOUNG WOMAN [*Indicating silks and saris in the hands of a hopeful merchant*]. **Oh, put them on, Marsinah!**

SECOND YOUNG WOMAN. **Yes, try them on!**

MARSINAH. **Shall I?**

Taking this as agreement, the young women escort MARSINAH *toward an enclosed booth. As soon as she is out of sight,* OMAR *plucks at the sleeve of the* CALIPH *who stands motionless, gazing after her.*

OMAR. **Enough, All Highest, enough. You'll be late.**

CALIPH [*Softly, still watching the booth*]. **Possibly, most possibly. In fact, most certainly.**

OMAR. **All highest, I have never seen that expression on your face before. It's sickening!** [*Impatiently*]. **Have you never seen a pretty face before?**

CALIPH. **Never—and I thought I'd seen thousands. Weren't you watching her?**

OMAR. No. When you're old and have no teeth there's no sense working up an appetite. Come, All Highest, important matters await you.

CALIPH. Important matters ? How goes that stanza of yours ?
"Ah love! Could you and I with Him conspire
To grasp this sorry scheme of things entire,
Would not we shatter it to bits—
And then remould it nearer to the heart's desire ? "

OMAR [*Judiciously*]. There's an ancient rule to be followed by men who fall in love: when you fall in love in Baghdad, get thee to Damascus. When you fall in love in Damascus—[*He makes a circular gesture and smiles reminiscently*]. Before I was called the Tentmaker, I used to be known as Omar the Traveller.

MARSINAH emerges from the booth. The townswomen gasp in delight at her delicate finery. They run to her side and lead her into a dance that suggests the exultation felt by a young girl wearing a new and lovely costume. The onlookers accompany the dance with song.

ALL [*Sung*] Ah! Ah!
Baubles, bangles,
Hear how they jing, jing-a-ling-a,
Baubles, bangles,
Bright shiny beads.

Sparkles, spangles,
My heart will sing, sing-a-ling-a,
Wearing baubles, bangles and beads.

MARSINAH I'll glitter and gleam so,
Make somebody dream so
That someday he may
Buy me a ring, ring-a-ling-a
I've heard that's where it leads—

ALL That's where it leads,
Wearing amulets, necklaces,
Stars in one's hair !

MARSINAH Wearing baubles, bangles—
[*She gives coins to BANGLEMAN*]
And beads !

She starts to leave. The CALIPH follows her, ignoring OMAR's sleeve-plucking. As the lights dim down, the last thing we see is the BANGLEMAN looking off after them. He seems to have a pretty good idea what he's started. He intones softly:

BANGLEMAN Baubles !—Bangles !—And beads !

D

SCENE 4

A narrow side street in Baghdad. Two of the WAZIR'S *policemen are gaming idly at dice. A busy little man who ekes out a horrid living as a police informer hurries in.*

INFORMER [*Excitedly*]. **Wazir's police! Wazir's police!**
FIRST POLICEMAN [*Engrossed in the dice*]. **What do you want?**
INFORMER. **I claim informer's fee.**

MUSIC No. 13—THE POET AND THE SLAVE GIRLS
(under dialogue)

FIRST POLICEMAN. **Against whom?**
INFORMER [*Enjoying his moment*]. **Jawan the brigand! He's here in Baghdad!**

Both policemen jump to their feet.

FIRST POLICEMAN. **How do you know?**
INFORMER. **I saw him pass in the street.**
FIRST POLICEMAN [*Tensely, to his subordinate*]. **Spread the word! Tell all patrols to travel in fours! Hasten!**

The SECOND POLICEMAN *runs out. The* FIRST POLICEMAN *beckons to the informer.*

You come with me to the Chief Janissary.

As they leave, THE POET *enters from the opposite direction. He lolls upon a richly cushioned litter that is carried by four callipygous and deliciously underclad* SLAVE GIRLS. THE POET *has bought himself a jewelled turban, a tunic of cloth of gold, and a mahogany hookah on which he puffs smugly.*

THE POET [*With eager solicitude*]. **Would you like to rest a while, ladies? I don't want to weary you.** [*They gently put the litter down*]. **Thank you. You did that very nicely.**
SLAVE GIRLS. **Thaa-ank you, Master.**
THE POET [*Determined to be a popular employer*]. **Frankly, I have never owned slaves before. I'm a bit vague as to what your rights are . . . ?**
SLAVE GIRL. **We have none, Master. Your word is our law.**
THE POET [*Sighing happily*]. **Then we certainly won't have any trouble getting along!**

THE POET *claps hands.* SLAVE GIRL *gets up and starts playing Lute.*

MUSIC No. 14—SLAVE GIRL SOLO

A SLAVE GIRL. **Where will we live, Master? Where is your palace?**
THE POET. **My palace?** [*He snickers*]. **I can see you're the practical one. My palace!** [*The thought convulses him*]. **Any other questions?**
SLAVE GIRLS. **Yes, where *is* your palace.**
THE POET. **As a matter of fact, my daughter is even now purchasing a lovely home just north of the pomegranate grove. You'll be quite comfortable there.**
A SLAVE GIRL. **You're so sweet, Master. If I weren't a slave, I'd kiss you.**
THE POET. **My dear girl, feel free to express your gratitude at all times! One thing I won't have around my house is class distinction.** [*Becoming confidential*]. **After all, I'm no high muck-a-muck myself.**
FIRST SLAVE GIRL [*Incredulously*]. **Aren't you even a Prince?**
SECOND SLAVE GIRL. **Or an Emir?**

THIRD SLAVE GIRL. **Or a noble ?**

FOURTH SLAVE GIRL. **What are you ?**

THE POET. **Ladies, I am a poet.** [*The girls groan*]. **Don't be disappointed yet—you haven't even heard my poetry. Listen . . . this one is called, " When Fortune Frowns."** [*The girls applaud mechanically. He scowls*]. **Not yet ! That's only the title !**

[*He recites with feeling :*]

The eyebrows of morning are arched in surprise,
Astounded anew that I should arise . . .

SLAVE GIRLS [*As he pauses to take a breath*]. **Now, Master ?**

THE POET [*Giving up*]. **All right—now.** [*He shrugs philosophically as the girls resume their mechanical applause*]. **After all, if I'd wanted poetry lovers, I could have bought poetry lovers. Rested now, girls ? Shall we go ?**

The CHIEF POLICEMAN *enters leading a squad of his men. At the sight of the policemen, the* SLAVE GIRLS *huddle behind* THE POET *in terror.*

SLAVE GIRLS. **The Wazir's police !**

THE POET [*With the confidence of wealth*]. **Be not alarmed. These fine constables can want nothing from well-to-do citizens.**

CHIEF POLICEMAN. **Nothing but your name, good sir.**

THE POET. **My name ? My name is . . .** [*He stops suddenly*]. **Why do you ask ?**

CHIEF POLICEMAN. **A bandit walks the city. We must challenge all identities.**

THE POET [*Indicating his rich clothing*]. **Gentlemen, do I look like a bandit ?**

CHIEF POLICEMAN [*Polite but firm*]. **If you can't identify yourself, we shall have to take you to the Wazir.**

THE POET [*Producing his purse*]. **Let us see if we cannot avoid that inconvenience. Shall we say one piece of gold for each of you ?**

The CHIEF POLICEMAN'S *eyes narrow and he grabs the purse.*

No ! Not the whole thing !

CHIEF POLICEMAN. **You acknowledge possession ?**

THE POET [*With fervour*]. **Officer, let there not be the slightest misunderstanding.** *That—is—my—purse !*

CHIEF POLICEMAN [*Bellowing*]. **Then why does it bear the print of the House of Achmed ?**

THE POET [*Stunned*]. **The print of what ?**

CHIEF POLICEMAN. **The House of Achmed—looted by robbers this last moon !** [*To his men*]. **Seize him !**

THE POET [*As they clap manacles on his wrists*]. **But *I* didn't steal it ! Jawan will admit he gave me the money for . . .**

CHIEF POLICEMAN [*Interrupting fiercely*]. **Jawan ! What about Jawan ?**

THE POET [*Appalled at his slip*]. **Did I say Jawan ?** [*Weakly*]. **Why did I say Jawan ?**

CHIEF POLICEMAN. **Consorting with Jawan, the brigand, eh ?** [*To his men*]. **Impound those slaves with the rest of this stolen property.**

SLAVE GIRLS. **Oh, no ! No !**

THE POET [*Miserably*]. **Gentlemen, you are making a hideous error !**

CHIEF POLICEMAN. **Lying thief ! The Wazir will have the truth out of you !**

He snaps his fingers. THE POET *and his possessions, animate and inanimate, are dragged down the street* THE POET *shakes one manacled fist toward the heavens.*

MUSIC No. 15—THE POET'S ARREST—PARADISE GARDEN
(under dialogue)

THE POET.   Oh Allah, how often in one day? How often will you give and take away? Why put me to all this trouble if I am to end as I started? [*He winces from a blow across his back, and gives vent to his misery in verse*].

> Oh, Allah, Buddha, and Confucius
> Bearers of Fate's golden cup,
> If everything is written down
> What's the use of getting up?

Allah, Buddha, and Confucius make no reply.   THE POET *staggers out.*

SCENE 5

A charming garden surrounding the Widow Yussef's house—premises MARSINAH *has long coveted. The garden is enclosed by a stone wall, and features a flowering mulberry tree.* MARSINAH *enters through a gate and sighs with delight as she surveys the garden. She hurries to the house and raps on the door. It is opened by a crochety male servant.*

MUSIC No. 15 (contd.)

SERVANT [*Shortly*]. **Peace be with you.**
MARSINAH. **Peace be with you. It is said that this house is for sale ?**
SERVANT. **I am only a servant.**
MARSINAH. **But it *is* for sale ?**
SERVANT. **Yes, it is for sale. Talk to the Widow Yussef when she returns.**
MARSINAH. **Thank you.** [*He starts to close the door but* MARSINAH *has another question*]. **Oh— is the roof sound ?**
SERVANT. **No.**

He closes the door in her face. Alone, MARSINAH *looks up at the roof. Then she shrugs and prowls about the garden.*

MARSINAH [*Lightly; talking to herself*]. **But it's so pretty !**

She pauses, the homemaker, and considers a shady area of the garden.

A little table in that corner . . .

She purses her lips thoughtfully. Unseen by her, OMAR *and the* CALIPH *appear at the gate behind her. The* CALIPH *motions* OMAR *away and quietly enters the garden.* MARSINAH *continues to soliloquize.*

. . . and over there father could plant a bed of hyacinths.

She shakes her head and smiles ruefully.

. . . well, *I* could. Father will have his own chair, with a sunshade, where he can sit and grow old peacefully. Every day at noon I'll bring him his grandchildren—for one hour, no more . . . they're such noisy, *active* children . . .

She turns slightly and sees the CALIPH. *She blinks at him, surprised but unalarmed.*

CALIPH [*Gently*]. **Do you often talk to yourself ?**
MARSINAH [*Reflecting*]. **Come to think of it—yes.**
CALIPH [*Smiling*]. **I do too. I've been told it's a sign of weakness.**
MARSINAH [*Quietly*]. **I've always thought it a sign of loneliness.**
CALIPH. **I think that is true.**

He moves towards her. MARSINAH *halts him with a gesture.*

MARSINAH. **I don't suppose you care, but you just stepped on my youngest child. A girl.**
CALIPH [*Solemnly*]. **She looks like you.**
MARSINAH. **People always tell me that.**
CALIPH. **She has her father's nose.**
MARSINAH [*Frowning*]. **Her father ?**
CALIPH. **Why do you let her eat pebbles ? Can't be good for her.**
MARSINAH. **I've told her and told her— she just won't listen.**
CALIPH. **Where is her father ?** [*He smiles*].
MARSINAH [*Glibly*]. **Off at work, of course. He's a—a gardner.** [*She breaks off and gazes candidly at him*]. **Like most things I love, he doesn't exist.**

29

CALIPH. **I know. Most things I love don't exist either.**

They look at each other silently.

About—about your daughter's father. You say he's a gardener. I happen to be a gardener too.

He reaches out and tentatively touches her hand. She pulls it away.

I'm sorry.

MUSIC No. 16—" STRANGER IN PARADISE "

MARSINAH [*Spoken—After a moment, puzzled*]. **I don't know why I moved my hand away. I didn't want to.**

Slowly she puts her hand back in his. He leans forward and touches his lips to hers. A long second passes. MARSINAH *turns her head and gazes at the garden as though seeing it for the first time.*

MARSINAH [*Singing*]

Oh, why do the leaves of the mulberry tree
   whisper diff'rently now ?
And why is the nightingale singing at noon
   on the mulberry bough ?
For some most mysterious reason
This isn't the garden I know . . .
No, it's Paradise now that was only a garden
   a moment ago !

CALIPH [*Singing*] Take my hand,
I'm a stranger in Paradise
All lost in a wonderland,
A stranger in Paradise.

If I stand starry-eyed,
That's a danger in Paradise
For mortals who stand beside
An angel like you.

I saw your face
And I ascended
Out of the commonplace
Into the rare !
Somewhere in space
I hang suspended
Until I know
There's a chance that you care;
Won't you answer the fervent prayer
Of a stranger in Paradise ?
Don't send me in dark despair
From all that I hunger for,

But open your angel's arms
To the stranger in Paradise
And tell him that he need be
A stranger no more.

She is in his arms at the end of the song.
Music continues under dialogue.

MARSINAH [*Spoken—Breaking away*]. **You say—you say you're a gardener. What kind of flowers should I plant along the fence ?**

CALIPH. **I must go in a moment—will you meet me here again this evening ?**

MARSINAH. **I thought hyacinths—but perhaps oleanders . . .**

CALIPH [*Insistently*]. **At moonrise ? Here in the garden ?**

MARSINAH [*Facing him again*]. **Yes.** [*Simply*]. **Yes, of course.**

CALIPH. **You won't forget ? You won't fail me ?**

MARSINAH [*Singing directly to him*]
>I saw your face
>And I ascended
>Out of the commonplace
>Into the rare!

CALIPH AND MARSINAH
>Somewhere in space
>I hang suspended . .

MARSINAH
>Until I know
>There's a chance that you care;
>Won't you answer the fervent prayer
>Of a stranger in Paradise?

CALIPH
>Don't send me in dark despair
>From all that I hunger for . . .

CALIPH AND MARSINAH
>But open your angel's arms
>To the stranger in Paradise
>And tell me that I need be
>A stranger no more!

They embrace. He turns swiftly and exits. MARSINAH
follows to the gate and gazes after him as the lights dim out

SCENE 6

MUSIC No. 17—THE ABABUS GO SHOPPING

A street not far from the Bazaar. Several vendors display their goods; music is playing softly as THE THREE PRINCESSES OF ABABU *enter attended by the* CHIEF POLICEMAN *and assorted members of the* WAZIR's *household. They are laden with the purchases of their shopping expedition. In dance pantomime, the smallest of* THE PRINCESSES *examines the wares of the first vendor, discovers a cobra in a basket, and decides for some private reason, best left unplumbed, to buy it. She wheedles the money from her sisters, and makes the purchase. The group proceeds to the next vendor. Their attention is distracted from his merchandise by the advent of a veiled woman in a travelling cloak. Her name is* PRINCESS ZUBBEDIYA OF DAMASCUS. *She is attended by a plump* AYAH *who carries a bit of parchment which she presents questioningly to one of the pedlars.*

PEDLAR [*Reading the parchment*]. **The Wazir's Palace?** [*To his fellows*]. **They want to go to the Wazir's Palace!** [*Turns to the* AYAH *again*]. **The black palace on top of the hill. You can't miss it—unless you're lucky.**

The AYAH *bows her thanks and leads her charge in the indicated direction. A townswoman gazes after them appraisingly.*

TOWNSWOMAN. **Look, another candidate for our Caliph's hand.**
SECOND TOWNSWOMAN. **Yes, they keep coming from all over.**

THE PRINCESSES re-act electrically to this news. They take the thought of competition with extreme displeasure.

FIRST PRINCESS [*Sharply, to her sisters*]. **Luul! Astaramoff aluul!**
SECOND PRINCESS. **Nevbah cacalamash.**
THIRD PRINCESS [*Explosively*]. **Splod!**
CHIEF POLICEMAN. [*Frightened; trying to mollify them*]. **Splod? Oh, please, ladies, don't be upset! Who could compete with you?**

As though in answer to his question, a second veiled charmer arrives. She is PRINCESS SAMARIS OF BANGALORE. *Her* AYAH *also has an address on a slip of parchment, but before she can present it, the pedlar points off, anticipating her request.*

PEDLAR. **Wazir's Palace? Straight up the hill!**

SAMARIS *and her* AYAH *bow and continue out as* THE PRINCESSES *glower at the* CHIEF POLICEMAN.

THIRD PRINCESS. **You sure Caliph want us?**
CHIEF POLICEMAN. **Beyond all doubt, Princess! Even now he stands at his window praying for a glimpse of you. Ladies, your beauty shines like a thousand lamps! Your skin is like the finest silk!**

THE PRINCESSES look dubiously at each other's skin; while they are thus engaged, the CALIPH, *still incognito, enters with* OMAR *in tow.* OMAR *halts, but the* CALIPH *continues walking.*

OMAR. **My boy, the litter is to meet us here.**
CALIPH [*His mind on his own problems*]. **Omar, how many concubines have I?**
OMAR. **Sixteen.**
CALIPH. **Get rid of them all. Give them presents, blessings, freedom—but get rid of them quickly.**
OMAR. **My poor boy! Would it not be wise to save somebody for a rainy day?**

CALIPH [*Loud enough to be heard by all*]. **Omar, I have fallen in love!
I should think that would be plain!**

MUSIC No. 18—" HE'S IN LOVE "

The sound of a drum precedes the entrance of the CALIPH'S *litter, accompanied by guards and attendants. Crying "The Caliph! The All Highest!", etc., the townspeople fall to their knees and remain thus until the* CALIPH *mounts the litter and is carried off. As he passes* THE PRINCESSES *they preen themselves flirtatiously—and get no response whatever.*

FIRST PRINCESS [*Spoken—Pointing angrily at the departing* CALIPH]. **Caliph sleem tistil!**

SECOND PRINCESS. **Caliph gleeb ruuy!**

THIRD PRINCESS [*Stamping her foot*]. **Caliph splod!**

The CHIEF POLICEMAN *is momentarily at a loss how to cope with their rage. A nugget of gossip from one of the townswomen gives him a straw to clutch.*

TOWNSWOMAN. **I heard him say he was in love.**

CHIEF POLICEMAN [*To* THE PRINCESSES]. **There, you hear? He is in love! Do not be misled by his shyness; he is timid, overcome by the sight of your beauty!** [*Pointing in the direction of the litter*]. **Look, his head is in the clouds!**

SECOND POLICEMAN [*Also pointing toward the off-stage* CALIPH, *and singing as convincingly as he can manage*]

  **See him smiling,
  Hear him humming,
  He's in love!
  Joyful, jaunty,
  Dreaming, dazzled,
  He's in love!**

ALL POLICEMEN **Stars have invaded his eyes,
  Silver bells in his voice
  Sing a hymn to the her he dreams of!**

CHIEF POLICEMAN **Watch him wooing.**

THIRD POLICEMAN **Purring, cooing.**

ALL **He's a dove!**

SECOND POLICEMAN

  **Sighing, doting,
  Flying, floating**

ALL. **High above!**

SECOND POLICEMAN

  **Though you're suspecting
  It's April affecting him so,**

ALL. **No,
  Can't be, can't be,
  Not him, not he,
  He's in love, and it's
  Really love, because
  I'm in love and I know!**

The CHIEF POLICEMAN *summons the two young swains who danced with* THE PRINCESSES *in the Bazaar. Once more the two young men and the three princesses dance, as onlookers take up the policemen's song—and once more* THE PRINCESSES *become obsessed with other thoughts than leaving Baghdad*

POLICEMEN AND TOWNSPEOPLE [*Sing*]

  **See him smiling
  Hear him humming
  He's in love!
  Joyful, jaunty,
  Dreaming, dazzled,
  He's in love!**

E

Stars have invaded his eyes
Silver bells in his voice
Sing a hymn to the her he dreams of!
Watch him wooing,
Purring, cooing,
He's a dove!

Sighing, doting,
Flying, floating
High above!

Though you're suspecting
It's April affecting him so
No,
Can't be, can't be,
Not him, not he,
He's in love, and it's
Really love, because
I'm in love and I know!
I'm in love and I know!

ACT 1 SCENE 7

SCENE 7

MUSIC No. 19—THE WAZIR'S PALACE

The throne room of His Exalted Excellency, the WAZIR OF POLICE *is a handsome, if forbidding, greenish-black hall with grilled windows. The* WAZIR *paces angrily in front of a massive throne-chair. He is scowling ferociously at letter in his hands.* LALUME *saunters in. Music stops.*

LALUME. You sent for me?

WAZIR [*Waving the letter*]. Lalume, our troubles are growing like bamboo shoots!

LALUME. My only trouble is boredom. Nothing seems to relieve it. [*With a glance at her husband*]. Nothing in sight, that is.

WAZIR. Really? And will it bore you further to learn our ten camel loads of gold are jeopardized?

LALUME [*Stretching out voluptuously on some pillows beside the throne*]. Insanely. But go ahead.

WAZIR. Claimants for the Caliph's hand are arriving from everywhere! Like locusts! If your three princesses fail me, I'll probably have to kill myself.

LALUME. My dear husband, you will never have to kill yourself!

WAZIR. Most humorous! Most amusing! Hah! [*Sharply to* CHIEF POLICEMAN *who stands to one side*]. Let the court of justice convene!

CHIEF POLICEMAN [*Calling toward the antechamber*]. The evening court of justice convenes!

The throne room begins to fill with officials, guards, prosecutors and prosecuted.

The evening court of the Wazir convenes! Silence and obedience, the court begins its meditations!

MUSIC No. 20—THE WAZIR'S COUNCIL

The Chief Policeman unrolls a scroll and reads.

The case of the seller of candlesticks, Ibn Nuwas, charged with breaking the pottery pots of Ali Dahdoud.

PROSECUTOR [*Stepping forward*]. Oh, illustrious Wazir, Ibn Nuwas pleads for a postponement of judgment until his broken legs are mended. He fell off of a pillow while being questioned.

WAZIR [*Amused*]. Next case.

CHIEF POLICEMAN. The case of Hajj the Beggar, charged with the theft of a hundred pieces of gold.

WAZIR. Let him appear.

SECOND POLICEMAN [*Calling off*]. Bring forth Hajj the Beggar!

Guards drag in THE POET *whose new finery is now disarranged and torn. He is thrust sprawling before the* WAZIR.

THE POET [*From his knees*]. At last—good fortune returns to me.

PROSECUTOR. Good fortune?

THE POET. The noble Wazir himself, sitting in judgment! Who could ask for a more righteous, a fairer, a finer judge?

WAZIR [*Annoyed*]. I loathe fawning beggars.

LALUME. He doesn't look like a beggar.

THE POET [*To* LALUME, *instantly*]. Before your loveliness, oh, Princess, every man is a beggar!

CHIEF POLICEMAN. Silence!

LALUME [*Smiling at* THE POET]. Oh, let him chatter a bit.

36

CHIEF POLICEMAN.   **The evidence against this criminal is as follows ...**

WAZIR [*Scowling from* LALUME *to* THE POET].   I need no evidence—one look was enough!   Under the laws of Baghdad, I order that the right hand of this liar, rogue and thief be cut off.

CHIEF POLICEMAN [*To* THE POET].   Have you aught to say before sentence is executed?

THE POET.   That I am a liar, I am not a big enough liar to deny. That I am a rogue can be verified by consulting anyone who knows me. And that I am a thief is as true as if it were writ in the Koran.   But, in this particular case—and, I may say, for the first time in my life— I am innocent.

WAZIR.   I dislike being mocked in public.   Add twenty lashes to my judgment.

CHIEF POLICEMAN [*To* THE POET].   Are you done with your protest?

THE POET.   It is rather expensive—but I should like to continue. [*Approaching the* WAZIR].   I can well understand your indifference to the fact that I am innocent, oh, Dispenser of Justice.   I, the pickpurse, the brawler, the seducer of women—innocent?   I can hardly believe my own ears.

LALUME.   Tell me, what sort of women did you prey upon?

THE POET [*Bowing elaborately*].   Until I beheld you, my memory of them was that they were all beautiful.

WAZIR.   It's his *tongue* that should be cut off!   But, let the sentence stand.   Right hand, off!

THE POET.   Oh, noble Wazir!   I assure you that I despise innocence as much as you.   It is at best a temporary state.

WAZIR.   Then what are you bothering me about?

THE POET.   The small matter of my losing my right hand!   Were I merely a beggar and thief, noble Wazir, I would not dispute your sentence.   A man can steal with one hand as well as with two.   And as for begging, he's better off with no hands at all.   But as a poet and story teller, the loss of a hand would cripple my career!

WAZIR [*Pointing to his own mouth*].   I am leaving you your mouth, scoundrel!

THE POET.   Hold!   [*He imitates the* WAZIR'S *gesture*].   For that simple sentence you needed your hand.   It is the gesture that tells the story. Let me convince you ...

LALUME [*As the* WAZIR *hesitates*].   Oh let him.   I love being convinced.

> The WAZIR *grunts ungraciously, but signals* THE POET *to proceed.*   THE POET *flexes his fingers, and the music starts.*

MUSIC No. 21—"GESTICULATE"

WAZIR [*Singing as he watches* THE POET'S *preparations*]
>   The things a merciful and clement Wazir must
>   endure!

LALUME [*Singing, her eyes on* THE POET]
>   How surely one can tell the expert from the
>   amateur!

THE POET [*Holding up his right hand and addressing it in song*]
>   Dear hand, deft hand,
>   Clever and facile extremity
>   Fond companion to me,
>   From my birth;
>   Sweet hand, swift hand,
>   Spinner of fable and fantasy,
>   Faithful friend of my art,
>   Would they rend us apart
>   Leaving no finger or fist there,
>   But just the hint of a wrist there?
>   Where then my spirited wit,
>   My mercurial charm?

                              Am I fated to sit
                              With an elbow, an arm
                              And no digits to top them off,
                              If they lop them off!

WAZIR'S COUNCIL [*Singing*]
                              Well said a plea as ever moved a man to shed
                                  a tear!
                              Well said, but not said well enough if we know
                                  our Wazir!

THE POET [*Singing directly to the* WAZIR]
                              How could I plead with you,
                              How could I pray to you?
                              How intercede with you,
                              What could I say to you?

WAZIR.   This is becoming a bore!

THE POET [*Pleadingly, demonstrating how he will look with no hand*]
                              Like a dog with no tail . . .

WAZIR.   . . . Drag this debris out the door!

                                                    Guards move to obey.

THE POET [*Struggling*]
                              Like a spoutless whale,
                              Like an elephant, sunk
                              If you cut off his trunk!

WAZIR   A bore! A bore! So do as I ordered before!

WAZIR'S COUNCIL   Drag this debris out the door!
                              Drag this debris out the door!

LALUME [*Her voice rising above the uproar*]
                              Hold!
                              I'd like to hear a little more!

The guards look toward the WAZIR *for instruction; he
shrugs and gestures that his wife is to have her way. The
guards unhand* THE POET *who genuflects to* LALUME.
*He removes his tunic, freeing his arms for further
gesturing.*

THE POET   When you tell a story,
                              Amorous or gory,
                              You can tell it best
                              If you gesticulate!

                                        Pantomimes the following with agile gestures.

                              Suppose the mighty Sinbad
                              Meets a Djinn who's been bad—
                              They will guess the rest
                              If you gesticulate!
                              A tongue is a tongue
                              And a lung is a lung
                              And a tale they can shout or sing;
                              Without the gesture—nothing!

WAZIR'S COUNCIL   Nothing!

THE POET   Should Sheherazade
                              Undulate her body,
                              That can be expressed
                              If you ges—
                              Can be assessed
                              If you ges—
                              She'll be undressed
                              If you gesticulate!

                              *He folds his arms, rendering his hands motionless, and
                              sings to the* WAZIR'S COUNCIL:

                              If I tell you I was walking by the sea
                              And found a Genie in a bottle,
                              That's trite.

WAZIR'S COUNCIL   Quite!
                              For practically everyone has seen a Genie

	Someone had to throttle
	In a bottle!
THE POET	Right!

He releases his hands and gestures extravagantly throughout the remainder of the song.

	But if
	I say
	The bottle
	Was sooooo teenie!
WAZIR'S COUNCIL	Sooooo teenie!
THE POET	And sooooo was the Genie!—
WAZIR'S COUNCIL	Sooooo was the Genie!
THE POET	—Until with trembling hand
	I pulled the cork! [*Council gasp*]
	And threw the jug and covered up my eyes!
	And the smoke began to curl—
WAZIR'S COUNCIL	[*Fascinated by his vivid gestures*]
	Ooh!
THE POET	And the smoke began to swirl—
WAZIR'S COUNCIL	Ooh!
THE POET	And it swirled and it curled
	And it curled and it swirled
	As higher it did rise,
	Till it was soooooo high!

The WAZIR'S COUNCIL *is entirely with him now, watching every motion with eyes wide, repeating his phrases after him:*

WAZIR'S COUNCIL	Sooooo high!
THE POET	And sooooo was the Genie!
WAZIR'S COUNCIL	And sooooo was the Genie!
THE POET	Then two great arms reached down—
WAZIR'S COUNCIL	[*Fearfully*]
	Two great arms?
THE POET	And lifted me up! Up! Up!
WAZIR'S COUNCIL	Up! Up! Up!
THE POET	Into the sky.
WAZIR'S COUNCIL	So high! So high!
THE POET	And we did fly,—
WAZIR'S COUNCIL	And he did fly!
THE POET	The Genie and I,
WAZIR'S COUNCIL	How he did fly!
THE POET	We did sail!
WAZIR'S COUNCIL	Did sail!
THE POET [*Asking the* WAZIR'S COUNCIL]	
	Is this a tale?
WAZIR'S COUNCIL	This *is* a tale!!
THE POET	Are you convinced?
WAZIR'S COUNCIL	We *are* convinced!
THE POET [*To the* WAZIR]	
	You see?
WAZIR'S COUNCIL [*To the* WAZIR]	
	You see? You see? You see?
THE POET	For the facile finger
	Listeners will linger;
	They will be impressed
	If you ges—
	Applaud with zest
	If you ges—
	If it's a question
	Of a story gory,
	Sinbad in bad,
	Bottle, smoke, Genie, arms,

> Fly—sky—high—I state,
> Reiterate,

THE POET AND THE COUNCIL
> Gesticulaaate—

THE POET   With your hands!
WAZIR'S COUNCIL   With your hands!

> *He falls to his knees before the* WAZIR; *all are silent as they wait for the verdict.* LALUME *glances at her husband.*

LALUME [*To the* WAZIR].   Rather clever, you must admit.

WAZIR [*Rising and crossing to* THE POET].   Too clever! I'm sure he has stolen far more than a hundred pieces of gold! [*Roaring down at* THE POET *who still kneels*]. Where have you hidden all the rest of the money?

THE POET.   Great Sir, believe me, I have stolen nothing!

WAZIR.   Another twenty lashes for that lie!

THE POET.   What money I have was paid me for lifting a curse from a man's head!

WAZIR.   You presume to have that power?

THE POET.   The power of prayer is infinite, Great Wazir—and I pray exceedingly well!

WAZIR [*To* CHIEF POLICEMAN].   Send men to his home. Bring me all who are there— all his confederates.

THE POET [*Quickly*].   No! There is no one at my home, no one at all! —Only a wretched, half-mad daughter—ugly, crackle-voiced. Please, she has done no wrong!

WAZIR [*Excited; waving* CHIEF POLICEMAN *to do as ordered*].   We have touched a sore spot! We are on the trail now! Go! Hurry!

CHIEF POLICEMAN [*Threateningly approaching* THE POET].   Where is your home?

> THE POET *hesitates—and then shakes his head firmly.*

WAZIR.   Execute the sentence!

THE POET [*He fights fiercely as guards grab him. With great violence he shouts at the* WAZIR].   May Allah curse you! May calamity strike you! May disaster overwhelm you! May you be driven from this palace and kicked into the road—A curse on your head! A curse on the head of the Wazir of Police!

> *The* WAZIR *sneers at this impotent curse. A sudden commotion postpones* THE POET'S *doom. Two guards enter, holding a struggling* JAWAN *between them. They hurl him to the floor.*

FIRST GUARD [*Breathlessly*].   Exalted Wazir, we have captured Jawan!

SECOND GUARD [*As a murmur of excitement fills the throne room*].   ...Jawan, the brigand, the robber, the assasin!

FIRST GUARD.   ...We've caught him at last!

> JAWAN *lifts his head from the floor, and looks around. He catches sight of* THE POET, *and gives a cry of rage.*

JAWAN.   There he is—the cheat! The pretender of powers! Let me tear out his liver! Let me rip his belly to ribbons! [*Guards hold him back*]. He removed a curse from me—for a hundred gold pieces. He swore I would find my son before the day was out! [*To* THE POET]. Where, you lying dog of a thief? Where is my son?

> *The* WAZIR *laughs delightedly.*

WAZIR [*To* THE POET].   So, you earned the money honestly, did you? A curse remover are you?

> JAWAN'S *attention has been diverted to the* WAZIR. *The old man lets out a shriek of ecstasy.*

JAWAN [*At the top of his lungs*].   Allah be praised! Allah is merciful, and Mohammed is his prophet! [*Pointing a shaking finger at the* WAZIR]. Look! That amulet! Oh Wazir, answer an old man one question— where did you get that amulet?

WAZIR.   This amulet has been with me since childhood.

JAWAN [*Tenderly holding out his manacled arms*].   I have found you! Ali, my little Ali!

WAZIR [*Frowning from* JAWAN *to* THE POET].   What does this mean?

JAWAN [*Tottering toward the* WAZIR].   I am your father! Ali, light of my soul, I hung that amulet about your tiny neck with my own hands one week before you were kidnapped . . . [*Fumbling in the depths of his shirt*]. Here, look, the other half! See how they match!

> *Wonderingly, the* WAZIR *fits the two amulet pieces together. After a moment he looks up, his eyes meeting* THE POET'S.

WAZIR [*Awed*].   They fit perfectly!

THE POET [*Matter-of-factly*].   Yes, of course.

WAZIR.   Allah be praised! A magician-beggar! A man with the power to curse and un-curse!

THE POET [*Regally*].   Have the kindness to bid your menials release me.

> *The* WAZIR *nods to* THE POET'S *captors.   They step back obediently.*

JAWAN [*Tearfully, to the* WAZIR'S *back*].   Speak to me! My father's heart aches for a word from its son!

WAZIR.   I'll attend to you in a moment . . . [*To* CHIEF POLICEMAN].   Call a recess.

CHIEF POLICEMAN [*Calling*].   Clear the court!

> *The ensemble starts out.   A guard shoves* THE POET *toward the door.*

WAZIR [*To* THE POET'S *guard*].   Let him remain!

> *The guard bows, and retreats.*

JAWAN.   What a wondrous end to my years of searching! Allah be thanked!

WAZIR [*Turning to him abruptly*].   You are Jawan, the robber and murderer? Is that true?

JAWAN [*Blissfully*].   Yes, yes! I am too overcome to speak more.

WAZIR.   You have said enough. You have confessed to being a criminal of the worst sort. [*To remaining police*].   Take him to the dungeons and dispose of him.

JAWAN.   But I am your father!

WAZIR [*Logically*].   All the more reason to be rid of you. For the leading judge of Mesopotamia to have as a father the leading criminal of Mesopotamia—it's a disturbing thought.

JAWAN.   Let me hear something from my son's lips other than a sentence to death!

WAZIR [*Affronted*].   Were you a true father, you would be proud of my integrity. [*Signalling the guards*].   To the dungeons with him!

JAWAN [*As he is hauled out*].   All I ask is one kind word from Ali—my little Ali . . .

WAZIR.   Goodbye!

> *He is gone.   There is a moment of somewhat embarrassed silence.*

THE POET.   Never have I seen a more touching reconciliation!

WAZIR [*To* LALUME].   We can use this man.

LALUME [*With private meaning*].   Yes. Yes, I rather think so.

> *The* WAZIR *stares thoughtfully at* THE POET.   *Then he suddenly slaps his thigh and gives a great shout.*

WAZIR.   Wait! Wait! Oh what an idiot I am!

> *He grabs a sword from a guard and advances murderously toward* THE POET *who steps back, alarmed.*

Of course the man's a fraud! Did he not place a curse on my head, with all the venom he could summon?

> *Jamming the sword into* THE POET'S *ribs.*

What became of that curse?

F

MUSIC No. 22—THE CALIPH'S NEWS—FANFARE I

Before THE POET *can answer, a gong sounds from the direction of the antechamber. One of the* CALIPH'S *heralds enters.*

HERALD. **Let all mouths close but mine! Let all mouths close but mine!**

All present sink to their knees.

The Holy, the Good, the Wise, the Just, the Omnipotent, the Commander of the Faithful, Menone al Raschid Ben Mohammed Ibn Khasimoun— the Caliph!

MUSIC No. 22 (contd.)—FANFARE II

The CALIPH *strides in. He is now dressed in full regalia.*

CALIPH [*Exuding happiness and goodwill*]. **Rise, my friends. Rise and rejoice!**

WAZIR [*Humbly*]. **Even the walls of my chambers rejoice at Your Highness's presence.**

CALIPH. **Your Caliph rejoices at the tidings he brings. He is pleased to notify his Wazir that he has chosen a bride. See that the proper proclamations are made. Tell the foreign embassies that their candidates for the Caliph's hand may return to their homes.** [*He beams at all, unconscious of the stricken expression on the* WAZIR'S *face*]. **May every citizen share his Caliph's happiness!**

MUSIC No. 22 (contd.)—FANFARE III

He sweeps out. The WAZIR *lets a moan of misery escape him.*

WAZIR. **Ruined!** [*Turning his back to the rest of the room and covering his face*]. **Hopelessly, utterly, gracelessly ruined!**

He lets his sword fall to the floor with a clatter.

LALUME [*To the attendants*]. **Leave us!**

Her eyes rove toward THE POET, *much curiosity in her expression. He quietly re-dons his tunic, and starts to sidle out.*

WAZIR. **Star-crossed! Why? Why should I be so accursed?** ... [*His voice trails away. He jumps to his feet and yells:*] **The beggar!** Who has put this wicked spell upon me? Who

THE POET realizes it is too late to escape. He stops and looks nonchalant. The WAZIR *points a shaking finger at him.*

You! It's you who did this!

THE POET airily inspects his fingernails and permits himself a modest shrug. The WAZIR *whirls and shouts to an off-stage functionary.*

Reverse my decision in the case of Hajj the Beggar! Restore his property!

FUNCTIONARY'S VOICE [*From off-stage*]. **Yes, Great Wazir!**

THE POET bows slightly to express his thanks. The WAZIR *crosses to him.*

WAZIR. **Now, quickly—let's settle the terms. A hundred pieces of gold was the price of your service to my deplorable parent?**

THE POET [*Regarding the doorway longingly*]. **Noble Wazir, my powers are depleted. Look what I have already done in one day. You must see I can do no more.**

LALUME. **Not even if we raise you to the rank of Emir?**

THE POET [*Overwhelmed*]. **Emir! Me—an Emir?**

WAZIR. **Lalume, an Emir is second only to me!**

LALUME. **Don't haggle with the wizard. He may take offence and turn you into something worse than you are.**

WAZIR [*Turning to* THE POET *again*].   You will be Hajj, Emir of Baghdad —if you prevent the Caliph's marriage.

THE POET [*Stammering*].   Prevent!   You are too kind . . . it is overwhelming.   What a day!   How can one possibly refuse such an offer— and yet, how in the world can one accept it ?

WAZIR.   You can't doubt your power ?

THE POET.   Indeed I can!   In fact, each time it functions, I am more and more astonished!

WAZIR.   Still it *does* function—I have seen it.

THE POET.   Yes, it does, doesn't it ?   [*He reaches a decision*].   Very well, noble Wazir, I accept your offer!

WAZIR.   [*Clapping his hands in satisfaction*].   Done!

CHIEF POLICEMAN [*Hurrying in*].   Excellency, a committee of your creditors awaits.

> The WAZIR *sighs and starts out gloomily.   Suddenly he stops and brightens.*

WAZIR [*To* THE POET, *beaming*].   A few minutes ago that would have worried me!

> *Jaunty now, chuckling to himself, he follows the* CHIEF POLICEMAN *out.   Alone with* THE POET, LALUME *sinks down onto the throne.*

LALUME [*Throatily*].   Come here.

> THE POET *glances around to make certain no one else is present.   He goes to the foot of the throne and pauses there.   She gestures for him to come closer; he does so.*

You dunce!   You're no more magician than I am!   The Wazir will drop you from a battlement onto a hook when he discovers you're a fraud.

THE POET.   Then may I make a suggestion ?   Let's not tell him.

LALUME.   He doesn't need to be told.   He'll know the moment the Caliph marries.

THE POET.   Love is a most uncertain business—even a Caliph's love. If he changes his mind, if they have a quarrel like young lovers do, why then—I am an Emir!   If not—well, that is Kismet.

LALUME.   And you'd gamble your life on such a slim chance ?

THE POET.   Princess, I have risked floggings for a handful of dates. I have courted the executioner to steal my dinner.   I have lived with fear too long and for too little, to let her terrify me now when the stakes are so great.

LALUME.   I despise recklessness, but I find myself admiring you.

THE POET.   Princess— I do too.   [*Emboldened, he sits beside her*].

LALUME [*Softly, after a moment*].   I've always had a weakness for scoundrels.

THE POET.   We are well matched.

> *They kiss with considerable enthusiasm.   While they are embraced two burly guards enter, one of them carrying* THE POET'S *pouch of gold.   They stop short and stare at the amorous tableau on the throne.*

FIRST GUARD [*To his companion*].   What kind of sentence did *he* get ?

> LALUME *and* THE POET *jump apart; the guard tosses the gold to* THE POET *who catches it.   The* WAZIR *enters, leading a bevy of his prettiest harem girls.*

WAZIR [*Beamishly, pointing to* THE POET].   There he is, my fine expensive harem!   There's your Emir-to-be!   [*To* THE POET].   They want to know you, maker-of-curses.   Your powers fascinate them.   [*To the girls*].   Go to him, ladies!   Don't be afraid, go to him!   [*To* THE POET, *smirking*].   Enjoy yourself, enjoy yourself!   Choose one— choose two. The supply is practically inexhaustible.

> *From the streets below comes the sound of much singing and jollification.   The harem girls rush to the windows to look out; other women of the household run in and hurry to the windows.*

WAZIR [*Roaring irritably*]. **What in hell's name is that commotion?**
GIRLS [*Peering out the windows*]. **It's the Caliph! It's his bridal procession!**
WAZIR. **What?** [*Turns on* THE POET]. **Begin your magic, Emir! It's the Caliph on his way to fetch his bride!**
THE POET. **Are you certain?**
WAZIR [*His suspicions aroused again*]. **Why are you disturbed? Didn't you promise you could prevent this marriage?**
THE POET. **Yes, but I didn't know you meant today!**
WAZIR. **Today, tomorrow, a month hence ... what's the difference? You're a magician, aren't you?** [*To the hubbub at the window*]. **Stop that noise, you caterwauling trulls!** [*To the* POET]. **Well? Are you going to keep your bargain?**
THE POET. **I—I doubt whether I have enough magic left for such a task.**
WAZIR. **Perhaps this will be a spur to your powers!** [*Roaring*]. **Guards! As soon as the wedding trumpets sound for the Caliph, I order you, without further ado, to** *skewer* **this reluctant magician!**

The guards draw their swords and scimitars.

Watch him carefully!

THE POET *swallows dryly, starts to speak, and then thinks better of it. He steps to the centre of the room and begins to make elaborate marks on the floor.*

What are you doing?
THE POET. **Shhh! I am calling on my powers!** [*He motions the women of the harem closer*]. **Assist me, all of you!**

LALUME *suppresses a smile and leads the harem women in assuming attitudes of mystical concentration.* THE POET *strokes his forehead and begins to speak, softly:*

Oh ye, who weaves at your tanglesome skeins
And daily spins the tapestry of agony and joy
That mortals call the history of man—
Cup thy ear to Hajj the Beggar!
LALUME AND HAREM WOMEN [*In hushed tones*]. **Shabash! Shabash!**

A harem girl gives vent to wails of superstitious ecstacy.

THE POET. Poor humans we, suspended between abyss and infinity—

MUSIC No. 23—"FATE"—FINALE ACT I

Lost in the shadows of yesterdays,
Ensnared in a labyrinth of tomorrows—
Help us! Help us!
LALUME AND HAREM GIRLS
Help us! Help us!

Several girls are swaying rhythmically, going into a trance.

THE POET [*Faster now, edging toward a door, as other girls wail*]
Below and above and in the swirling darkness—
Of the infinity of mind and matter
There is a plan that only thou can see and only thou control!
We ask then that from the woof and warp
Of history yet unborn
The marriage of our Caliph be noiselessly extracted!
LALUME AND HAREM GIRLS
Shabash!
THE POET
Remove our Caliph's love for this woman,
Or remove the woman from our Caliph—
It is thy choice!

LALUME AND HAREM GIRLS [*As one girl screams and a deep drum rolls*]
   Shabash!

All now move rhythmically as the drum begins an insistent and accelerating beat. Several of the girls writhe in frenzies of mysticism.

THE POET [*Spoken—Edging closer to the door—only to find it well guarded by police with scimitars*]

  Goat of Mendes! Baphomet!
  Blight and blast our Caliph's love!
  Twice this day hast thou seen
  Fit to grant what I ween

  Twice this day hast thou let
  Hajj's humble prayer
  Climb up heaven's stair,
  And Kismet so ordained
  My goal should be attained!
  Another prayer, another cry,
  Grant again, grant it, I
  Ask thee now, ask thee now,
  Kismet, mystery of fate!

A general scream, another drum-roll, and then dead silence. He has them in his power. He sings, edging toward another door:

  Fate, heed me as I lower my knee,
  A beggar begging your ear
  To hear his plea!
  Fate, let the sound of my voice beguile,
  Look with love on your slave below
  And show your smile!

  'Tis but a trifle I ask,
  That in the master design
  Which you have written and sealed
  You change one line:

This door too is guarded. THE POET *returns to where* LALUME *is leading the harem in a wild trance dance.*

  This love that mustn't be—
  This he, this she—
  Turn her smile into scorn,
  Turn his heart into stone,
  Turn the honey on their lips to brine!
  Then, Fate, the day is mine!

He pantomimes to LALUME *that the only possible exit is the window. She blows him a kiss for luck; he drops his cloak to the floor, threads his way through the swirling, unseeing dancers, climbs out onto a ledge outside the window and disappears. The wild dance and incantations continue for a moment and then the* WAZIR *sees* THE POET'S *discarded cloak. He grabs it, looks around for* THE POET *and discovers he has vanished. The* WAZIR *hurries to* LALUME *and, with a gesture, asks where the man has gone.* LALUME *points straight up. At this manifestation of supernatural power, the* WAZIR *hurls himself to his knees and makes obeisance in rhythm to the trance music.*

End of Act I

CURTAIN

MUSIC No. 24—ENTR'ACTE

ACT II—SCENE 1

MUSIC No. 25—"NIGHT OF MY NIGHTS"

A street in the neighbourhood of the Widow Yussef's house.
It is just before moonrise. The evening is filled with music from the CALIPH'S *nearby nuptial procession. Dancing girls appear waving garlands of spring flowers to perfume the air for their approaching ruler. The girls are followed by lute players in white and gold array.* OMAR, *busily and tipsily in charge of proceedings, enters with the* CALIPH *who is resplendent in a white wedding costume.*

ORDER OF PROCESSION.
(1) Singing Ladies; (2) Lute Player; (3) Dancers; (4) Caliph and Omar; (5) Lynn and Jude; (6) Beggars; (7) Townswomen; (8) Litter, 2 Policemen, Chief Policeman; (9) Merchants; (10) Dancing Girls and Boys.

OMAR [*Spoken, over music*]. Now, the royal carpet is to be laid from the litter to the steps of her house—and the musicians are to stand well back. Turn left at the end of the byway, then go straight ahead. Swing wide of the camel stable.

CALIPH. Omar, you're taking the long way around!

OMAR. Be patient, Almighty Bridegroom—no one in your family ever married in this district before. [*He chuckles at the* CALIPH'S *eagerness*]. Will you give the orders to resume the procession?

CALIPH [*Singing to the members of the procession*]
> Play on the cymbal, the timbal, the lyre,
> Play with appropriate passion; Fashion
> Songs of delight and delicious desire
> For the night of my nights!
>
> Come where the so well beloved is waiting,
> Where the rose and the jasmine mingle,
> While I tell her the moon is for mating
> And 'tis sin to be single!
>
> Let peacocks and monkeys in purple adornings
> Show her the way to my bridal chamber,
> Then get you gone till the morn of my mornings
> After the night of my nights!

The entourage now joins him in his song.

CALIPH	GIRLS	MEN
After the night of my nights	Ah! Ah!	Ah! Ah!
'Tis the night of my nights!	Ah! Ah!	Ah! Ah!
Ah!	Bng! Bng!	Play on the cymbal, the timbal, the lyre,
	Bng! Bng!	Play with appropriate passion; Fashion
	Fashion	
	Songs of delight and delicious desire.	Songs of delight and delicious desire.
For the night of my nights!	Hm . . .	
		Come where the so well beloved is waiting,
	Hm . . .	Where the rose and the jasmine mingle,
		While I tell her the
	Hm . . .	moon is for mating.

46

And 'tis sin to be single!

Hm ... Hm ...
Let peacocks and
  monkeys in purple
  adornings
Show her the way to
  my! Ah!
Get you gone till the
  morn of my mornings

Let peacocks and monkeys
  in purple adornings

Show her the way to my
  bridal chamber
Then get you gone till
  the morn of my mornings

After the night of my nights!

After the night of my
  nights!

After the night of my
  nights!

'Tis the night of my nights!
'Tis the night of my nights!

After the night of my
  nights!

After the night of my
  nights!

More girls enter, bearing an ivory litter designed to convey the CALIPH's bride to his palace. They are followed by richly garbed functionaries who carry a long tapestried carpet—for the feet of the CALIPH's bride must not be soiled by contact with the ground.

Now it is almost moonrise and a servant hands to the CALIPH a plain gardener's cloak. The CALIPH dons this and leads the procession off. As the last of the entourage disappears, the CALIPH's exultant song still hovers in the distance.

SCENE 2

MUSIC No. 26—" STRANGER IN PARADISE "—REPRISE

The Garden. A few lights from the house cause the garden to glow gently in the darkness. MARSINAH *enters and stands by the gate for a moment, smiling at the scene of her first lovers' rendezvous and listening as she seems to hear the music of their meeting.*

MARSINAH [*Singing softly*]
. . . And why is the nightingale singing at noon
on the mulberry bough ?

She pauses, remembering.

No, it's Paradise now that was only a garden
a moment ago !

Take my hand,
I'm a stranger in Paradise,
All lost in a wonderland,
A stranger in Paradise.

If I stand starry-eyed,
That's a danger in Paradise
For mortals who stand beside
An angel like you.

She is distracted from her song by the distant strains of the procession. Puzzled, she climbs up on a bench and peers curiously in the direction of the music. While she is thus engrossed, THE POET *hurries in. Music continues under dialogue.*

THE POET. Marsinah, thank heavens ! I've looked everywhere !
MARSINAH [*Pointing off*]. Look, Father, a state procession ! Musicians, dancers . . .

She breaks off, remembering she has not seen her father since morning. A similar thought occurs to THE POET. *Music fades.*

THE POET AND MARSINAH [*Together*]. Where have you been ?

But THE POET *has no time for domestic accounting. He pulls* MARSINAH *down from the bench and speaks urgently.*

THE POET. My darling, this is important . . . [*Handing her the pouch of gold*]. Here is what's left of our gold—ninety-one pieces, ample to buy your living for many years. Keep ten for your dowry so that you can marry a man of substance. And keep still another ten hidden somewhere, just in case your husband should be cruel or mean.
MARSINAH. Now what are you up to ? What intricate scheme this time ?
THE POET [*Gravely*]. Go to the grain shop by the East gate. Hide there till tomorrow's caravan leaves for Damascus . . .
MARSINAH [*Startled*]. Damascus ?
THE POET. . . . Wait for me at the inn there. Within a week I'll come for you. If I don't—forget me. Which is a father's way of saying, remember me kindly and with love.
MARSINAH [*Sympathetically*]. My poor father—some angry husband again ?
THE POET [*Explaining rapidly*]. If by any wonderful chance the Caliph doesn't marry his commoner, I'll be an Emir and you an Emir's daughter. Otherwise, I will have made a great and powerful enemy. The Wazir of the Police.

The sounds of the wedding procession continue to grow louder.

48

MARSINAH. **The Wazir.**

THE POET. **He would destroy you as well as me. Go now, my darling.**

MARSINAH [*Shaking her head*]. **No! No, I won't leave you!** [*She casts an anxious glance toward the gate*]. **Father, everything that's dear to me is here—you, our nice little corner of the camel stable . . .**

THE POET. **And everything that's dear to me will be in Damascus! Time is running out—go, my love.**

MARSINAH [*Coaxing*]. **I've never disobeyed you . . . I'll leave in just a little while. Just after moonrise.**

THE POET. **At any moment we may hear the Caliph's wedding trumpets! You must go before they sound!**

MARSINAH. **But there is someone I promised to meet here.**

THE POET [*His temper rising*]. **She can wait! Now, go!**

MARSINAH. **No!**

THE POET. **Marsinah, this is life or death—*your* life or death! Do as I say!**

MARSINAH. **I can't I—I won't!**

He raises his hand to strike her, a gesture so foreign to him that it startles him almost as much as it does MARSINAH. *She stares at his raised hand in disbelief. He lowers it slowly.* MARSINAH *swallows a sob, then turns and runs out. For a miserable instant,* THE POET *watches her go. He slaps his thigh angrily, and dashes out in the opposite direction. A second later the members of the wedding procession appear in the gateway. Two functionaries put the ceremonial carpet in place. The* CALIPH *glances around the garden, seeing that his beloved has apparently not yet arrived.*

CALIPH [*To his entourage*]. **Now conceal yourselves, friends! Conceal yourselves until this signal!**

He shows them a large silver box. It is brimming with jewels. He slams its lid loudly to demonstrate.

OMAR [*Weaving a bit as he regards the carpet*]. **Oh, the carpet from the litter has fallen short!** [*Wagging his head*]. **How sad when royalty tries to achieve the superhuman. Let the carpet fall a little short—result, royalty is merely human after all. My boy, as you go through life remember this: it's the little bit on the end that counts!**

He suddenly becomes aware of the jewel box in the CALIPH'S *hands. He blinks at it woozily.*

What have you there? The bridal jewels! You've gone weak witted! Those jewels haven't left the Palace in hundreds of years!

CALIPH [*As fatuous as any bridegroom*]. **She adores baubles. These will make her smile.**

OMAR [*Dryly*]. **What a simple, unaffected girl she must be!**

He leaves the garden, and joins the other members of the entourage in concealment nearby.

MUSIC No. 27—BAUBLES, BANGLES AND BEADS—REPRISE

Alone, the CALIPH *gazes tenderly toward the house that he imagines to contain his beloved. He signals to off-stage Lute Player and sings softly:*

CALIPH.   Baubles, bangles,
               Hear how they jing, jing-a-ling-a,
               Baubles, bangles,
               Bright shiny beads!

The door of the house opens and a veiled woman emerges. Believing this to be MARSINAH, *the* CALIPH *opens the jewel box and extends it toward her. The woman inspects it with interest.*

G

WOMAN [*In a flat, middle-aged voice*].   **Very pretty.   How much are they?**
CALIPH [*Appalled*].   **What!**
WOMAN.   **You pedlars!**

The CALIPH *yanks the veil from her face.   She screams in alarm and retreats.*

A veil snatcher!   Police, police!

OMAR *hears her shouts and appears in the gateway.*

CALIPH [*To the woman*].   **Be not alarmed ...**

He removes his cloak revealing his official vestments. The woman gasps and drops to her knees.

WOMAN.   **The All Highest!   Forgive me, oh, forgive me!**
CALIPH [*Gently, raising her up*].   **The fault is mine, Madam.   I seek a young girl who lives here.   Your sister, perhaps, or a cousin?**
WOMAN.   **No one lives here but me.   I'm a widow.**
CALIPH.   **But I recall this house—that tree.   She stood there this very morning.**
WOMAN [*Recalling*].   **Was she a pretty young girl?**
CALIPH.   **Yes, yes!**
WOMAN.   **She's someone who wants to buy this house.**
CALIPH [*Eagerly*].   **What is her name?**
WOMAN.   **She never said.   But I saw her just a moment ago from the window ...**
CALIPH.   **Here?**
WOMAN [*Nodding*].   **Yes.   She was talking with a man ...**   [*She breaks off, embarrassed*].
CALIPH.   **Speak frankly.**
WOMAN [*Reluctantly*].   **They talked—I saw him put his arms around her ... when I looked again—they were gone ...**

Stricken, the CALIPH *stares at her for a moment.   He turns away slowly.*

CALIPH [*To* OMAR].   **Reward her.**

OMAR *hands her coins.   She salaams, and retreats into her house.*

OMAR [*Softly, to the* CALIPH].   **Now, do you doubt the wisdom of your love?**
CALIPH [*Fiercely*].   **Never!   And the story that seems to damn her will have a clear and simple explanation!**
OMAR.   **Alas, it is only those who love well whom love can hurt.**

Unthinking, he punctuates his remark by slamming the lid of the jewel case.   In response to this pre-arranged signal, the entourage bursts out of hiding and dances in through the gate, singing riotously.

MUSIC No. 28—" HE'S IN LOVE "—REPRISE

ENTOURAGE.   See him smiling,
                Hear him humming,
                He's in love!
                Joyful, jaunty,
                Dreaming, dazzled,
                He's in love! ...
OMAR [*Running frantically among the singers*].   **No, no!   Quiet!   Stop! It's a mistake ...**   [*The singing comes to a ragged halt*].   **Friends, the young lady isn't here.   However, it is only a temporary disappointment and your Caliph would dislike to have it exaggerated by gossip.   Now go— and on your return to the Palace, sing your liveliest and celebrate loudly so that no one will know that the litter is empty!   But forgive me if I do not join you.**

MUSIC No. 29—THE EMPTY LITTER AND THE WAZIR'S SPIES

Obediently, the members of the procession resume their song as they gather up the carpet, pick up the litter, and depart.

ENTOURAGE [*Singing, as they exit*]

    Play on the cymbal, the timbal, the lyre,
    Play with appropriate passion; fashion
    Songs of delight and delicious desire,
    For the night of my nights!
    For the night of my nights!

CALIPH [*Singing ruefully*]

    'Tis the night of my nights!

He goes out, following the empty litter.
Music continues into next Scene.

SCENE 3

MUSIC No. 29 (contd.)

An anteroom to the WAZIR'S harem.
The CHIEF POLICEMAN is consulting with several small,
black cowled figures. LALUME, the WAZIR, and guards
enter.
Music fades.

CHIEF POLICEMAN. **Kneel, spies.** [*They do so. The* CHIEF POLICEMAN *bows to his master*]. **Your Exalted Excellency, spies from every quarter of the city. All bring the same message.**

WAZIR [*Despairingly*]. **I know, I heard the bridal procession returning to the Palace. They sounded happy. Oh, the miserable swine, they sounded happy!**

CHIEF POLICEMAN. **A subterfuge, My Lord. The Caliph hoped to conceal the fact that his commoner bride had disappeared.**

LALUME. **What? Impossible!**

WAZIR. **Allah be praised!**

LALUME. **How disappeared? Kidnapped? Murdered?**

CHIEF POLICEMAN. **Neither, Oh, Wife of Wives. Erased.** [*With a meaningful glance at the* WAZIR].

LALUME. **As though by wizardry?**

A SPY [*In assent*]. **Wizardry, indeed, Great Lady.**

WAZIR [*Ecstatic*]. **Wizardry! Of course, wizardry!** [*He pats the spy on the head rather as though he were petting a dog*]. **Good spy, faithful spy!** [*To the* CHIEF POLICEMAN]. **Take our loyal spies below, give them food, wine, a banquet! And give them the usual fee.** [*Unseen by the spies, he makes a private throat-cutting gesture to the* CHIEF POLICEMAN, *who nods and leads the spies out. The* WAZIR *turns to* LALUME]. **The beggar-wizard has saved me! All the gold ten camels can carry! There are a hundred uses for such a magician—a thousand! Lalume, we must ensure his loyalty. We must make him happy.**

LALUME. **I mean to try.**

WAZIR. **Prepare the rooftop pavilion. Scent it with attar of roses. Inform the harem to perform the Emir Induction Service, to delight him continuously—feed him sweetmeats and hasheesh! Feed him Rahadlakum!**

LALUME. **It shall be done, My Lord.**

WAZIR [*Impatient for all this beneficence to begin*]. **Where is he now? Why does he not return?**

LALUME. **He'll be back.**

WAZIR. **How can you be sure?**

LALUME. **You'd just be angry if I told you . . .**

She exits languidly. The WAZIR *frowns after her but quickly returns to his dreams of glory. He addresses the* CHIEF POLICEMAN *expansively.*

WAZIR. **Imagine the Wazir of Police with a wizard in his employ— power within power! How subtly I shall change the face of Baghdad! Subtlety, always subtlety . . . anyone can be violent and crude, but subtlety has put me where I am!**

MUSIC No. 30—"WAS I WAZIR?"

Mad with his own perfume, he sings. His guards march in cadence to his song:

When we caught the seven hundred men
And hung them in their prison pen,
Who said, suspend them by their fuzz—?
Was I Wazir? I was!

52

GUARDS	Was he Wazir ? He was !
WAZIR	When the keeper of the royal zoo
	Was short a cockatoo or two,
	Who sealed him in a pot of glue—?
	Was I Wazir ? I was !
GUARDS	Was he Wazir ? He was !
	He has a way of learning what he wants to know,
	Delicate, but to the point !
WAZIR	They always seem to remember
	When I begin to dismember them
	Arm by arm and ear by ear and joint by joint !
	When the court musician lost his grasp
	And let his lute begin to rasp
	Who had him bitten by an asp ?
	Was I Wazir ?
GUARDS	Was he Wazir ?
WAZIR	Was I Wazir ?
GUARDS	Was he Wazir ?
WAZIR	I was !
	The time we caught the man who said I wasn't
	nice—
GUARDS	Joy, oh joy,
	That was a time !
WAZIR	I confiscated his mother
	And then did something or other
	Involving her dissolving
	In a vat of lime !
	When at last, in manner neat and deft,
	I've hacked and hatcheted and cleft
	Until no one but me is left,
	I want it clear—
GUARDS	He wants it clear !
WAZIR	I *was* Wazir !
GUARDS	And *is* Wazir
	In every single charming
	And disarming
	Thing he does !
WAZIR	Was I Wazir ?
GUARDS	Wazir he was !
WAZIR [*Ad nauseam*]	
	I was !

The guards carry him out.

ACT II SCENE 4

SCENE 4

MUSIC No. 31—RAHADLAKUM

A terrace atop the WAZIR'S *harem. A sea of silken cushions suggests that the main occupation of a terrace-dweller is lying down. The pavilions of exquisite Persian design provide refuge for moments of privacy, or inclement weather. They are well separated from each other, and face in different directions. The scene is bathed in star-light and seductive music.*

THE POET *reclines blissfully upon a divan. He wears a new suit, although "suit" is hardly the word for a garment that Ptolemy I might have worn when taking his best girl for a walk on the Egyptian equivalent of Easter Sunday. Harem ladies, concubines, and dancing girls are devoting themselves to* THE POET'S *amusement. Clad in shimmering bits of cloth that accent their nudity, they dance for him, fan him, stroke his brow, proffer him salvers of fruit, wine, and sweetmeats.* THE POET *seems dizzied with delight.* LALUME *enters to begin the Emir's Induction Ceremony. She smiles at her guest, and addresses the girls.*

LALUME [*Spoken*]. **Ladies—shall we begin service ?**

The girls seem ready. They form an eager circle around the incipient Emir. LALUME *approaches him.*

What shall be the subject of our erotic discourse ?
THE POET [*Spoken—Eyeing the circle of avid femininity*]. **Shall we discuss the nature of—virtue ?**
LALUME [*Singing*] **Think, Ladies,**
　　　　　　Cogitate !
　　　　　　Sharpen up the edges of your wit !
A GIRL [*Speaking—after some thought*
　　　　　　Virtue is the purest lily Allah ever grew.
AN AYAH [*Spoken*]
　　　　　　Virtue is the spotless fruit upon the tree of
　　　　　　　　character.
LALUME [*Spoken, flatly*]
　　　　　　Virtue is its own reward.
THE POET [*Rising and singing*]
　　　　　　Virtue is the pathway to Paradise,
　　　　　　Virtue is the road from doom,
　　　　　　Virtue is the foe of depravity,

　　　　　　Barricade to Hell's dark cavity !
　　　　　　Virtue is the nectar celestial,
　　　　　　Virtue is divine perfume !
　　　　　　Virtue is the god's own ambrosia,
　　　　　　Virtue is—

A plump ayah runs in holding a steaming silver bowl of Rahadlakum, a variety of the confection otherwise known as Turkish delight.

AYAH [*Spoken—Finishing the sentence for* THE POET]
　　　　　　—Rahadlakum !
FOUR OF THE GIRLS [*Singing passionately as they stare at the bowl of candy*]
　　　　　　Ahhhhhhhhhhh !
LALUME [*Singing*] **Rahadlakum !**
THE POET [*Spoken—With incredulous delight*]
　　　　　　Rahadlakum ?

55

AYAH AND LALUME [*Sung—Insistently*]
                    Ra—had—la—kum !

                                        LALUME *beckons* THE POET *to her, and sings.*

LALUME   On days when my lord groweth restless
                And bored with his sword and his plume
                His handmaiden hath what he needeth,
                And what doth he need ?—
THE POET   —Rahadlakum !
LALUME   On nights when my lord looketh listless
                And black is the hue of his gloom
                His handmaiden hath what he lacketh,
                And what doth he lack ?—
THE POET   —Rahadlakum !
                    [*He sniffs the bowl of candy and sings with gusto*]
                'Tis sweet with the meat of the lichi nut
                Combined with the kumquat rind,
                The kind of confection
                To drive a man out of
                His Mesopotamian mind !
LALUME   And lo, if my lord feeleth faithless
                And roameth by night from his room
                His handmaiden fanneth her fires
                And out of her pan riseth a tantalizing perfume . . .
THE POET   He scenteth the scent,
                He turneth his face,
                His previous place in her embrace
                He doth resume !
THE POET AND LALUME [*Singing together*]
                And love is in bloom
                The while they consume
                Rahadlakum !
ALL   Rahadlakum !

                                *They crowd around the bowl helping themselves to the
                                confection, and bowing to the new Emir.
                                They all dance with mounting excitement.*

THE POET   He scenteth the scent
LALUME AND AYAH
                Ah-o-E' Ah-a   Ah-o E'-o
THE POET   He turneth his face
LALUME AND AYAH
                Ah-o E' Ah-o Ah-o E'-o!
THE POET   His previous place in her embrace
                He doth resume !
HAREM GIRLS   O-o-o Ah-o E'
THE POET AND LALUME
                And love is in bloom
HAREM GIRLS   Love is in bloom
THE POET AND LALUME
                The while they consume
HAREM GIRLS   The while they consume
THE POET   Ra-ha-ha- Ra-ha-ha
                Ra-ha-ha-ha-ha-
LALUME   Ra-ha-ha, Ra-ha-ha-ha-ha
AYAH   Ra-ha-ha, ha-ha
ALL   Rahadlakum !
LALUME [*Clapping her hands*].   Now leave us ! All of you !

                                The ladies leave. LALUME *sits on the divan, gesturing*
                                THE POET *to join her. As he does so, a* MANSERVANT
                                enters and salaams.

MANSERVANT. Oh, gracious new Emir, everyone marvels at your
wizardry. May an humble servant plead a benefit from your magic ?

THE POET [*Grandly, with a small wink to* LALUME]. **He may.**

MANSERVANT. **My third wife is soon to spawn a child. I now have seven daughters—will the gracious Emir this time grant me a boy?**

THE POET. **My good man, this assurance I can give you: if it is not a boy, it will not be my fault.**

MANSERVANT. **Oh, thank you, thank you!**

He bows himself out.

THE POET [*Fascinated by the thought*]. **Now, there's a source of income I hadn't considered—a sex arranger. No, that doesn't sound right. Gender fixer?** [*He shakes his head*]. **Too medical. Well, whatever you call it, it's a wonderful line of business. And fifty percent honest!**

LALUME. **You don't seem to realize that you have now been set above little business schemes, above poverty—above honesty.**

THE POET. **I was always above honesty.** [*A notion occurs to him*]. **And yet, have I not given full measure lately? Did not the Caliph's commoner disappear as I guaranteed? Did not Jawan find his son? Could it possibly be that I actually do possess the power...?** [*He stops short as he considers this possibility. He crosses to a pavilion wall, measures his height against it, and marks the spot with a finger as he turns his face toward heaven*]. **Allah, this is Hajj again. Make me three inches taller.** [*He steps back under his hand. His height has not altered. He shrugs lightly and returns to* LALUME]. **Where were we?**

LALUME. **Sex arranging, I believe.**

He brightens and moves closer to her.

THE POET. **The subject interests you?**

He strokes her arm. LALUME *casts an apprehensive glance over her shoulder.*

LALUME. **That husband of mine creeps around ... he's been trying to catch me for years. He never has, though!**

THE POET [*Shaking his head in reproof—but moving closer*]. **Oh, women, women! The authors, the inventors of sin!**

LALUME. **They say a bit of innocence lurks in all women, waiting for the right man to find it.**

THE POET. **I am most anxious to search.**

LALUME. **Not now! Not here!**

THE POET. **But when, Lalume? And where, Lalume? And in heaven's name how soon can we be there, Lalume?**

LALUME. **Well, I have heard of a certain oasis in the desert, about a week's journey away by dromedary. Not that I've ever been there, of course!**

THE POET. **Of course!**

LALUME. **It's called the Oasis of Delightful Imaginings ...**

Just thinking about this fabulous resort makes her sigh with delight, and close her eyes.

THE POET. [*Softly, putting his arm around her waist*]. **Tell me about it.**

LALUME. **No one around for miles and miles, no sound but the faint rustling of palm trees ...** [*He rustles a fan in his hand*] **... A warm desert wind caressing your skin ...** [*He caresses her skin and kisses her neck*] **... In the distance the cry of a wild camel ...**

A wild roar from the interior of the harem interrupts her.

WAZIR'S VOICE. **Lalume!**

THE POET *jumps away from* LALUME. *His guilty reflex causes him to dart behind the divan where he conceals himself as the* WAZIR *enters.*

WAZIR. **Lalume, why didn't you answer? They tell me Hajj has arrived.**

LALUME. **He left here a bare moment ago.**

WAZIR. **But I've been at the bottom of the stairs for *several* moments.**

LALUME. **You know he doesn't need to use stairs.**

WAZIR [*Shuddering*]. **Doesn't he give you a creepy feeling?**

LALUME. **You mean a sort of tingly sensation under the skin?** [*The*

H

WAZIR *nods*]. **He certainly does!**

WAZIR. **Well, I wish he'd come back.** [*Indicates jewelled crown in his hand*]. **I have his coronet here, but I can't wait all day.**

THE POET [*Appearing, like an apparition*]. **You were looking for me?**

WAZIR [*Jumping*]. **Urk!** [*He recovers and manages a thin smile*]. **Where did you come from?**

THE POET. **That would be hard to explain to a layman.**

WAZIR [*Placing the coronet on* THE POET'S *head*]. **Your Emirship, Your Emirship.**

THE POET **I thank you.**

WAZIR. **Everything satisfactory?**

THE POET. **Eminently!**

WAZIR. **Is there anything at all you want?**

THE POET [*With a sidelong glance at* LALUME]. **Nothing that is not within reach . . .**

WAZIR. **Well, call me in the harem if you want me. I'll be lying down.**

> *He goes out. A servant enters from another direction.*

SERVANT. **Your daughter, Glorious Emir.**

> MARSINAH *appears, and runs to her father. The servant leaves.*

MARSINAH. **Father! You're safe!**

THE POET [*Embracing her*]. **Of course, my darling. Why else would I send for you?** [*Presenting her to* LALUME]. **Lalume, this is my daughter, Marsinah. Marsinah, Lalume.** [*They acknowledge the introduction warily.* THE POET *preens himself*]. **Marsinah—notice anything?**

> *He models his coronet self-consciously.*

MARSINAH. **An Emir! You really are!** [THE POET *smirkes with pride*].

THE POET [*To* LALUME]. **Is there a place worthy of an Emir's daughter in the Palace?**

LALUME [*Starting out*]. **I shall arrange a lovely apartment in the women's quarters.**

MARSINAH. **Please don't trouble yourself.**

LALUME. **No trouble at all! Any child of Hajj's is a child of m . . .**

> *She checks herself, smiles foolishly and departs. As soon as they are alone,* MARSINAH *takes her father's hand.*

MARSINAH. **Father, I tried to tell you before . . . I didn't want to leave because I've fallen in love.**

THE POET [*Annoyed*]. **At a time like this you talk of some infantile infatuation?**

MARSINAH [*Gently*]. **It's love, Father—as real and as deep as the one I feel for you.**

THE POET [*Pacing angrily*]. **We'll keep you here until I find someone I can trust. Then I'll** *send* **you to Damascus!**

MARSINAH. **I'm sorry, but I won't go. I've lost him. I didn't know how much it mattered until I realized I'd never find him again— there's no way. I'm sorry . . .**

THE POET [*Gesturing inclusively at his surroundings*]. **This is all for you, you know, this grab for riches.** [MARSINAH *makes no comment.* THE POET *reflects a moment*]. **I suppose parents always say that.**

MARSINAH. **It** *is* **for me, I know. I must seem ungrateful, but . . .** [*She starts to cry*].

THE POET [*Scolding her tenderly*]. **Headstrong, disobedient . . . shh shh shh, my darling. Please don't cry.**

> *He pats her consolingly as she continues to weep. He leads her into a pavilion where they are out of sight and earshot from the events that follow on the terrace. The* CHIEF POLICEMAN *appears. He looks about, seeking the* WAZIR.

CHIELF POLICEMAN [*Calling*]. **Your Exalted Excellency!**

WAZIR'S VOICE [*From the interior of the harem*]. **Yes?**

CHIEF POLICEMAN. **Sir! Sir, the All Highest! He's here!**

WAZIR [*Running in*]. **Here? Are you certain?** [*The* CALIPH *appears. The* WAZIR *and* CHIEF POLICEMAN *drop to their knees*]. **All Highest! Welcome to my humble . . .**

CALIPH [*Brusquely*]. **Without delay, Wazir of Police, notify your entire force of the following assignment. They must find the girl, the girl your Caliph told you he was determined to marry. Are you ready to receive details?**

MUSIC No. 32—"AND THIS IS MY BELOVED"

WAZIR. **Yes, Sire. I, personally will dispose the forces.**

> *The* WAZIR *snaps his fingers to the* CHIEF POLICEMAN *who produces writing materials and takes notes as the* CALIPH *continues*

CALIPH. **I saw her first this noontime in the Bazaar of the Caravans. She was alone, purchasing clothing . . .**

> *The* CALIPH *has been striding back and forth nervously. His pacing takes him toward the second pavilion where the backs of the* WAZIR *and* CHIEF POLICEMAN *cut him off from view. His voice becomes inaudible. At this moment, lights come up in the first pavilion.* THE POET *is helping dry* MARSINAH'S *tears.*

THE POET [*Spoken over music, tenderly*]. **Now tell me about him. Who is he?**

MARSINAH. **He's a gardener—that's all I know!**

THE POET. **All right, I'll find him for you. Now—he's a gardener. Is he tall? Short?**

> [*He prompts her by* singing *softly*]
> **You'd say his eyes were— ?**

MARSINAH [*Responding in song*]
Sometime bright.

THE POET [*The musical interrogation continues*]
But only sometime?

MARSINAH [*Nodding*]
Often dark.

THE POET   **Well, that is plain!**

MARSINAH   **Plain words can't tell the thrill!**

THE POET   **Then tell it how you will!**

> *She rises and sings her description of her lover. At the same time the* CALIPH *moves away from the second pavilion, and his conversation with the* WAZIR *once more becomes audible. Like* THE POET, *the* WAZIR *is asking his questions musically, and like* MARSINAH, *the* CALIPH *finds his emotions are best expressed in melody. Thus a quartet is sung, each pair unaware of the presence of the other.*

MARSINAH	WAZIR
Dawn's promising skies,	**You'd say her eyes were— ?**
	CALIPH
	Sometime bright.
	WAZIR
Petals on a pool drifting;	**But only sometime?**
	CALIPH
	Often dark.
	WAZIR
Imagine these in one pair of eyes,	**Not very clear!**
	CALIPH
	Mere words cannot convey!
And this is my beloved!	
	WAZIR
	Then try another way.

THE POET
You'd say his smile was— ?
MARSINAH
Sometime gay.
THE POET
But only sometime ?

MARSINAH
Often sad.
THE POET
Sad smiles are strange !

MARSINAH
He can be very strange—
THE POET
So ?
MARSINAH
I hope he'll never change !

CALIPH
Strange spice from the south,

Honey through the comb
    sifting;

CALIPH
Imagine these on one eager
    mouth,
WAZIR
This takes imagining !
CALIPH
And this is my beloved !

WAZIR
And when she speaks ?
CALIPH
Ah !

THE POET
And when he talks to you ?
MARSINAH
Ah—
Mystery !

Music !

WAZIR
Music ?

THE POET
Mystery ?

And when he walks with
    you ?
MARSINAH
Paradise comes suddenly
    near !
THE POET
It's clear, it's love !
MARSINAH
All that can stir,
THE POET
Ill find your love !
MARSINAH
All that can stun,
THE POET
I promise you I will !
MARSINAH
All that's for the heart's lift-
    ing;
THE POET
Those eyes should never cry !
MARSINAH
Imagine these in one perfect
    one—
THE POET
With all my heart I'll try !

And when she moves

CALIPH
Paradise comes suddenly
    near !
WAZIR
I fear this love !
CALIPH
All that can stir,
WAZIR
All Highest One—
CALIPH
All that can stun,
WAZIR
—I offer so much more !
CALIPH
All that's for the heart's lift-
    ing;
WAZIR [Aside]
Hopeless !
CALIPH
Imagine these in one perfect
    one—
WAZIR [To CALIPH]
For every man there's more
    than one !
        [Aside]
We'll wait !
CALIPH
And this is my beloved !

MARSINAH
And this is my beloved!

The music continues softly under dialogue.

THE POET [*Gently kissing* MARSINAH'S *brow*]. **Don't worry. I'll find him for you. I promise.**

He goes out. At the same time the CALIPH *turns to leave, pausing to call over his shoulder to the* WAZIR.

CALIPH. **Now then, in heaven's name, start the search!**
WAZIR. **But, All Highest, the description is so vague . . .**
CALIPH. **Do not argue with me, Wazir! Start the search!**

He strides out, the WAZIR *following.* MARSINAH *stands alone in her pavilion, still gazing at the picture in her mind.*

MARSINAH [*Singing*]
            Dawn's promising skies,
            Petals on a pool drifting;
            Imagine these in one pair of eyes,
            And this is my beloved.

            And when he speaks—
            And when he talks to me—
            Music! Mystery!
            And when he moves
            And when he walks with me
            Paradise comes suddenly near!

            All that can stir,
            All that can stun,
            All that's for the heart's lifting;
            Imagine these in one perfect one,
            And this is my beloved!
            And this is my beloved!

SCENE 5

MUSIC No. 33—THE POETS MEET

A corridor in the WAZIR'S *Palace.* THE POET, *now bedecked in a trailing cape of peacock feathers, is attended by several young women of the harem. He is handing money to one of the* WAZIR'S *policemen.*

THE POET. Here, this will pay you for your trouble.

POLICEMAN. But, Emir, all I know about him is that he's a gardener and loves your daughter!

THE POET. Then bring me all young males carrying spades and wearing hang-dog expressions. Quickly, please.

POLICEMAN [*Confused*]. As you command, Great Emir.

He wanders out. Alone with his female attendants, THE POET *primps his clothing, snaps his fingers for a mirror. A girl hands him a little looking glass, while another girl shoves a high pedestal table under his elbow so that his arm will not suffer the small fatigue of holding the mirror. He gazes contentedly into the mirror, admiring himself in his coronet. Behind him,* OMAR *enters and pauses in surprise at this open display of egotism.* THE POET *catches sight of* OMAR *in the mirror and turns abruptly*

OMAR. You look vaguely familiar. Who are you?

THE POET [*Loftily, returning to contemplation of the mirror*]. In the immortal phrase of the student Al Bab el Benaar, who wants to know?

OMAR. I thought I knew every Emir in Baghdad. You must be a new one. Created by the Wazir?

THE POET [*Extemporizing*]

> The inquisitive nose
> Invading a crack
> Once cut off
> Can't be put back!

OMAR. A poet! That's a novelty in Emirs.

THE POET. A poet indeed! And one day the Caliph himself will hear my verses, and give the boot to that tenth-rate poet laureate he has the bad taste to admire.

OMAR. I wish you hadn't said that.

THE POET. Why so? Do you, too, admire him?

OMAR. No, but you see— I happen to *be* that tenth-rate poet laureate.

THE POET. You?

OMAR. Me.

THE POET [*Quoting contemptuously*]. " The moving finger writes, and, having writ, moves on? "

OMAR [*With a sigh*]. Repetitious?

THE POET. Trite! [*He stops, and shakes his head in self-reproof*]. Forgive me. But, you see, I was such an unsuccessful poet, and for so many years . . . Your pardon, please.

They smile at each other and shake hands.

OMAR. Tell me, what is a man of talent and feeling doing in the ménage of the Wazir of Police?

THE POET. At the moment, I am his magician.

OMAR. Do you plan to remain in his service?

THE POET. Only a fool would leave a barnyard where the goose is laying golden eggs.

OMAR. Which is the more foolish, the live fool or the dead fool?

THE POET. Fear not for me. I have conquered the danger.

OMAR [*Also extemporizing*].

> Here's a poem
> With sense and quickness:

62

Greed kills many
More than sickness.

THE POET. Greed! Yesterday my daughter and I were starving!

OMAR. Advice is never welcome. Still . . . [He points toward the WAZIR's throne room]. In that direction may lie wealth—but with it something terribly sudden. [He points in the opposite direction]. In this direction there is only a gate, but a gate through which the fool you mentioned might leave.

THE POET. Omar, my friend, there is always something to be learned—even from fools.

MUSIC No. 34—"THE OLIVE TREE"

[He sings his philosophy]

A fool sat beneath an olive tree
And a wondrous thought had he,
So he rose and he told it to the sky.
And where was I?
Behind the tree.
I overheard
His reverie:

" Why be content with an olive
When you could have the tree?
Why be content to be nothing
When there's nothing you couldn't be?
Why be contented with one olive tree
When you could have a whole olive grove?
Why be content with a grove
When you could have the world?"

The fool stood beneath the olive tree,
" What a wondrous thought," said he,
" But alas, it is very, very deep!"
And then he yawned
And went to sleep.
Because, you see,
He was a fool!

" Why be content with an olive
When you could have the tree?"
That which has lulled you to sleep, fool,
Has awakened me!
Why should I sigh that my lot is my lot,
That I can't make it anything more,
When this is a lie,
An excuse for a fool to snore!

I walked from behind the olive tree
With a wondrous change in me
For I walked with my eye upon a star!
If you have heard
And do not heed,
There is a word
For what you are,
And oh, my friend,
The word is " fool!"

He waves jauntily to OMAR, and strolls out in the direction of the WAZIR's throne room.

SCENE 6

MUSIC No. 35—THE WAZIR'S WEDDING

The anteroom of the WAZIR'S *harem. The* CALIPH *is speaking sharply to the* WAZIR.

CALIPH. You don't seem to understand. A royal marriage has been promised the people and a royal marriage there must be!

WAZIR. We will try, Highness, to find her. But permit me to say the delusion that you can be happy with one woman—it's a stage a man goes through. Will Your Highness be gracious enough to glance into my harem?

The CALIPH *shoots a disgusted look at him and the* WAZIR *hastily explains.*

I have a secret means of watching—a small device from which I have derived a great deal of innocent amusement.

He signals to the CHIEF POLICEMAN *who relays the signal to an unseen assistant. The wall of the harem chamber becomes transparent, revealing* THE THREE PRINCESSES OF ABABU. *They are bathing.*

The simple creatures don't know they're being observed. These are the three Princesses of Ababu. Note their charm and consider an alliance with them means a safe northern frontier, a . . .

CALIPH. I do not require your advice on military security!

He is about to turn away, offended at this peeping, when MARSINAH *appears in the harem chamber. The* CALIPH *stares at her in disbelief and dismay.*

WAZIR [*Oblivious, rambling on*]. If you will look again, Sire, it is not only military security I offer you. They, all three, have been trained to . . .

CALIPH [*A cry of pain*]. It is she! It is! There, the girl your Caliph seeks— in your harem!

The WAZIR *is nonplussed. He peers stupidly into the harem. Recovering his wits, he signals the* CHIEF POLICEMAN *and the transparent wall becomes opaque once more. The* CALIPH *buries his face in his hands.*

WAZIR. But that's impossible! Impossible! [*He whispers some hasty instructions to the* CHIEF POLICEMAN *who runs out. The* WAZIR *eyes the stunned* CALIPH *cautiously, and decides on an attitude. He takes the* CALIPH'S *arm with a great show of sympathy*]. All Highest, one marries so many people! Of course she can no longer become your wife, but if you'd like her as a concubine—please. With my most sincere compliments.

CALIPH. Concubine? No, Wazir, it was not a concubine I sought.

WAZIR. I pray Your Highness does not blame me for your disappointment.

CALIPH [*Evenly*]. Enough, Wazir! The incident is closed. Send your three princesses of—wherever it is—to the Caliph's Diwan tonight. Inform all embassies and missions to present their candidates for the Caliph's hand. This night he will choose a Wife of Wives! [*He goes out*].

WAZIR [*As soon as he is alone*]. Oh, my brilliant new Emir! He transferred the woman to my own harem!

The door of the harem chamber opens, and the CHIEF POLICEMAN *emerges, followed by* MARSINAH. *She is in the grasp of a burly guard who holds her cruelly, one great hand gagging her mouth. The* WAZIR *looks at her critically. She is fighting to free herself.*

The Caliph believes this female to be one of my wives—I would not
have him discover me in a lie. [*To the* CHIEF POLICEMAN]. Witness the
ceremony and enter it into the records as of a month ago. [*He spreads
a hand over* MARSINAH's *head, and makes an equivalent gesture above his own*].
Empowered as first judge of Baghdad to create and cause marriage
between two or more true believers of the faith, I officially accept this
creature as wife of the seventh rank. Now, be she mine. [MARSINAH
has redoubled her struggles. He bends towards her]. Congratulations! [*To
the* CHIEF POLICEMAN]. Have her scrubbed and anointed. I will visit her
after the Diwan tonight.

> *Guard starts to drag* MARSINAH *out. She manages to jerk
> her head free long enough to let out a defiant shout.*

    MARSINAH.   If you do, I'll kill myself! I swear it!

    WAZIR [*Brightening*]. Really ? Well, this may be the most interesting
bridal night I've had in years!

> *He regards her with interest as she is dragged away,
> squirming helplessly.*
> *Blackout.*

I

ACT II SCENE 7

SCENE 7

MUSIC No. 36—THE CALIPH'S DIWAN

The great ceremonial hall in the CALIPH'S *Palace. It features, amidst a parade of marble arches and columns, a large pool into which a fountain plays. The* CALIPH'S *Chair of State faces the pool.*
Baghdad's nobles move in sociable circles among the arches and columns. They are arrayed in glittering Oriental pomp. The reception, or Diwan, is about to commence. OMAR *appears and addresses the guests.*

OMAR. **Oh, nobles of Baghdad, flowers of Islam, now begins the Diwan of your Caliph's betrothal.**

The CALIPH *enters, expressionless and splendid. The assemblage makes obeisance.*

The Highest of the High!

The CALIPH *takes his place in the Chair of State, and indicates that his subjects may rise.* OMAR *opens a scroll and reads to the* CALIPH. *Music stops.*

Oh, Prince of True Believers, first of the enchanting maidens who aspires to the incredible honour of becoming your wife is the beauteous Zubbediya of Damascus. [*He puts the scroll down and consults his own libidinous imagination*]. **Alluring as the mirage—pulsing as the sirocco— agile as the mongoose! Zubbediya of Damascus!**

MUSIC No. 37—ZUBBEDIYA

A drum rhythm accompanies the entrance of dancing girls who carry a long silk shield toward the CALIPH. ZUBBEDIYA'S *plump ayah is the first to step from behind the shield. With great ceremony she unfolds a small rug, and places it on the floor in front of the* CALIPH. *Then, eyes rolling at the wonder of the loveliness she is about to present, she claps her hands. The dancing girls retreat, revealing* ZUBBEDIYA, *a proud and fiery beauty. The ayah removes a cloak from* ZUBBEDIYA'S *shoulders, unwinds her turban and palms a handful of* ZUBBEDIYA'S *rich hair toward the* CALIPH *as if it were jewellry of great price. Then she claps her hands and gives a shrill shout.* ZUBBEDIYA *begins to dance. As the beauty dances closer and closer to the* CALIPH, *the ayah, overcome with her charge's charms, beats her hands on the floor and delivers an excited chant in which only the word "*ZUBBEDIYA*" is comprehensible. The* CALIPH *watches the performance stonily. Prostrate at the conclusion of the dance,* ZUB-BEDIYA *is carried out by guards. The ayah scampers after her. Once more* OMAR *steps forward, consulting his scroll.*

MUSIC No. 38—SAMARIS' DANCE

And now, oh, Commander of the Faithful, permit me to call forth the second contestant for your noble heart—Samaris of Bangalore. Samaris of Bangalore will endeavour to captivate you with dances of her native India. Samaris of Bangalore!

The dancing girls re-enter with their silk shield. Aligned before the CALIPH, *they whisk it aside, and* SAMARIS *is revealed. She is costumed as a Hindu temple dancer and wears a headdress of ornate Indian design. She dances a precise, formalistic Hindu dance that describes, to the initiated, the marriage of her destiny to the* CALIPH'S *Her exit brings* OMAR *forward once more.*

67

And now, Great Caliph, the three Princesses of Ababu—[*He sees the* WAZIR *beckoning urgently and crosses to him. The* WAZIR *whispers briefly in his ear.* OMAR *shrugs acquiescence, and turns to the* CALIPH]. **Your Wazir wants me to remind you that, according to the Koran, he who looks through three windows sees more than one olive tree.** [*The* WAZIR *bows his thanks and* OMAR *proceeds*]. **So devoutly do these Princesses desire your happiness that they have put aside the natural rivalry of womankind, and each is prepared to marry that third of you which she can serve best.**

MUSIC No. 39—ABABU DANCE II

> *He salaams and steps back as the drums begin to beat a jungle rhythm.* THE THREE PRINCESSES *enter in single file, wearing the unlikely costumes of huntresses from the mountains of Ababu. Their dance is a pantomimed hunt that demonstrates to the* CALIPH *how they intend to keep his table bountifully supplied with wild game. As they exit, the* WAZIR *rises and nervously approaches his ruler.*

WAZIR.   Ah, the delight in your eyes shows your decision, oh, Fount of Wisdom! All Baghdad will rejoice—and all Ababu as well.

CALIPH [*Harshly*].   Your Caliph has made no decision. [*He turns to* OMAR]. A refinement of torture, Omar. Author of no crime, I must select my own punishment. Have you composed the cadence for which I asked? The cadence to prove the futility of love?

OMAR.   I have All Highest. Even Euclid could not prove it more conclusively [*He clears his throat; many of the guests step closer, better to hear the great man's poesy*].

MUSIC No. 40—FROM THE RUBAIYAT

> [*Spoken over music*].
> Come, fill the cup, and in the fire of Spring
> Your winter garment of despondence fling!
> The bird of time has but a little way
> To flutter—and the bird is on the wing!
> The world moves on, nothing won . . .

> *His tone drops as he moves closer to his ruler and aims his words at the* CALIPH'S *ears alone. Guests form a cluster around them. The* WAZIR, *agitated, edges away from the group and starts to pace.*

WAZIR [*As he passes* LALUME].   He's making me nervous!

> THE POET *enters, and approaches* LALUME, *his manner urgent.*

OMAR [*His voice diminishing*].
> . . . moves on! Nor all your deep regret nor wit
> Shall lure it back half a sun,
> Nor all your tears wash out a word of it!

> *He is now inaudible. His part of the stage becomes dark, allowing us to concentrate on* LALUME *and* THE POET.
> *Music stops.*

THE POET   Lalume, I've been looking everywhere for Marsinah!

LALUME   She must be in the women's quarters. I'll fetch her.

> *She departs. The* WAZIR *has seen* THE POET *and hurries toward him.*

WAZIR.   Hajj, my dear talented friend! [*Taking his arm possessively*]. Is it too late to put a curse on Samaris and Zubbediya?

THE POET.   Too late and too public.

WAZIR [*Glumly*].   Oh. [*Then, his spirits reviving*]. By the way, that was an ingenious feat of magic you performed today.

THE POET [*Elegantly adjusting his coronet*].   Which?

WAZIR.   Transferring the Caliph's beloved to my own harem.

THE POET [*Amazed*]. **What ?** [*Recovering*]. **Oh, just routine wizardry.**
WAZIR. **Wonderful, but you should have told me. I thought all was**
ost **when the Caliph saw her. But I told him the girl was my wife.**

He emphasizes his cleverness with a dig of the elbow.

THE POET. **What a jewelled brain !**
WAZIR. **. . . And then, just to protect myself, I married her.** [*Amused*].
She swore to kill herself tonight.
THE POET. **My poor friend, a most unflattering decision !**
WAZIR. **Angry little thing. Can't imagine what attracted the**
Caliph. What's her name ? [*Snaps fingers, trying to recall*]. **Marsinah !**
That's it, Marsinah !
THE POET [*Stunned*]. **Marsinah ? No !**
WAZIR. **Yes, Marsinah.**
THE POET [*To himself, staggered*]. **Allah, forgive me ! What have I**
done !
WAZIR [*Interpreting* THE POET'S *cry of pain as an apology*]. **Oh, that's all**
right. She won't be a danger to us very long—I had the dressmaker
sell her a phial of poison. [*He nods toward the* CALIPH]. **Look at him,**
descendant of Mohammed, outwitted by an ordinary mortal ! [*He has*
unwisely turned his back on THE POET *who draws a knife from a jewelled scabbard*].
It just goes to prove that owning a cloth-of-gold suit and a bathing pool
doesn't sharpen a man's mind !

MUSIC No. 40 (contd.)

THE POET, *about to plunge his knife into the* WAZIR'S *back hesitates and looks at the bathing pool. An inspiration seizes him. He returns the knife to its scabbard.*

With all his power he could not find her—and a few hours from now
she will have destroyed herself !

Lights come up on the CALIPH, *et al, and* OMAR'S *voice is heard finishing his recitation.*

OMAR.   **Some for the glories of this world**
             And some sigh for the Prophet's paradise to come
             . . . Ah, take the cash and let the credit go,
             Nor heed the rumble of a distant drum !

THE POET *strides toward the* CALIPH. *As he moves, he takes a shiny gold plaque, five or six inches in diameter, from his turban.*
Music stops.

THE POET [*Holding the plaque aloft*]. **Behold ! Behold, Mighty Caliph !**
CALIPH. **What have you there ?**
THE POET. **Only a bare plaque, All Highest !** [*He flashes it toward the*
guests in the manner of a professional magician]. **Look, My Lords and Ladies,**
no name is marked upon it.
WAZIR [*Aside, to* THE POET, *baffled*]. **What are you doing ? Be careful !**
THE POET [*Ignoring the* WAZIR; *to the guests and* CALIPH]. **I throw it thus—**
into the pool ! [*He throws the plaque into the pool. A murmur of interested*
comment arises from the onlookers]. **When fetched from the water, this magic**
plaque will be inscribed with the name of our Caliph's bride-to-be !

This promised diversion excites more comment; the guests move closer to the pool. THE POET *draws the* WAZIR *aside and produces a second plaque, exactly like the first. Keeping it hidden from all but the* WAZIR, *he scribbles on it with the point of his knife, and whispers to the* WAZIR.

Bring this one up out of the pool. Ababu is written upon it. Hide it
in your boot—quickly, or you'll spoil the trick !

Delighted by this stratagem, the WAZIR *seizes the plaque secretes it in his boot.* THE POET *turns to the* CALIPH.

Oh, Noble Caliph, lest you suspect fraud, your loyal Wazir himself will
retrieve the plaque.
OMAR. **The Wazir ?**

THE POET [*Firmly*].   Only he can serve the end I have in mind.

CALIPH.   Wazir, explain this fellow's arrogance!

WAZIR.   A man of wondrous magic, All Highest.   The most potent of wizards!

CALIPH.   You vouch for him?

WAZIR [*Trembling with eagerness*].   Great Caliph, if he be not the most reliable and talented soothsayer in Baghdad, may Allah strike me dead within the hour!

CALIPH [*Raising an eyebrow*].   A mighty oath for so casual a question.

WAZIR.   It was I who discovered him, Your Highness.   He never makes a mistake.   He is infallible!

CALIPH [*Indifferent*].   Proceed.

THE POET [*As the* WAZIR *crosses to the pool and starts to disrobe*].   Your indulgence, All Highest.   Too much light quarrels with my art.   May they smother the torches?

> The CALIPH *gestures his permission. The lights dim.* THE POET *moves to the* WAZIR, *places his hand on his shoulder, and indicates the pool.*

WAZIR [*All eagerness*].   Now?

THE POET [*Softly, trying to conceal the hatred in his eyes*].   Now.

> The WAZIR *gingerly puts a foot into the water;* THE POET *gives him an encouraging smile, and the* WAZIR *continues to immerse himself.* THE POET *faces the* CALIPH.

This trick may take a little while, Oh Most Tender of Lords.   [*A hasty aside to the* WAZIR, *who has paused in his descent*].   All the way to the bottom my brilliant assistant!   Have no fear—Hajj is here to help you!

> The WAZIR *resumes his progress.* THE POET *strikes a magicianly pose, and recites to the* CALIPH.

This feat, if you trouble to try,
Will assist you to understand
The infinite slowness of eye
Compared to the speed of the hand.

[*Aside to the* WAZIR]
Your foot!   Give me your foot!

> The WAZIR *is standing on the bottom now, only his moon-like face appearing above the parapet of the pool.*

WAZIR [*Stupidly*].   My foot?

> He *remembers the plaque in his boot, and starts to obey.* OMAR *steps forward and points a finger at* THE POET.

OMAR.   Now I know you!   You're the rhyming beggar who bargained with me on the steps of the mosque!

CALIPH [*Curiously*].   Who are you?   Beggar?   Emir?   Magician?

> The WAZIR *has laboriously raised one foot up to the parapet.* THE POET *gives him an approving smile, and then grabs the extended foot. He yanks it upward, the* WAZIR'S *head disappearing as he is up-ended in the pool.* THE POET *tucks the foot under his arm and holds it aloft with all his might. His face betrays nothing of the effort he is making to defeat the* WAZIR'S *titanic struggles. Calmly, he answers the* CALIPH'S *question.*

THE POET.   All of them and none of them, oh illustrious one!   I am a story teller.

[*He illustrates by reciting*]
My tale is a story of grief,
Of weird and unnatural sin
Of evil beyond all belief—
And it happened, this tale I spin!

> The WAZIR *gives a couple of monumental kicks, but* THE POET *hangs on, his unperturbed manner confirming the illusion that his magic feat is proceeding according to plan. He continues rhyming to the* CALIPH.

Oh descendant of Mohammet,
Of the whirlwind and the comet,
Will you venture us a verdict on a fiend ?
Will you condescend to trust us
With the way you'd render justice
To the most unhuman monster ever weaned ?

OMAR [*Peering into pool*]. He seems to be struggling. If I didn't
know you were a magician, I'd swear he was drowning !

THE POET [*With a merry laugh*]. Yes, he struggles well, doesn't he ?
All part of the illusion of course !

Hastily, as several guards take an unsure step forward.

Let me assure you, he is doing exactly what I wish him to do !

The guards retreat. THE POET *faces the* CALIPH *once more.*

Gentle ruler, be not angry when I say
Your subjects have been told your heart is broken—
Perhaps your heart has died !
What judgment would you pass, oh King,
If your love were lost because a lie were spoken ?
What judgment upon the man who lied ?

CALIPH. Why do you ask ? Whom do you accuse ?

THE POET. A lover of torture, a drinker of tears,
Who laughs aloud when the innocent weep
And to all beseechment turns stone deaf ears !
[*To the now motionless foot*]
Oh, drinker of tears, drink ! Drink deep !

CALIPH [*Rising, disturbed*]. Who is this man ? Name me his name ?

THE POET. A bargain, Great Caliph ! Name me his sentence first !

CALIPH [*Agrily*]. I would order his death without delay and without
mercy !

THE POET. I thank you for your verdict ! It has been carried out !

MUSIC No. 41—THE WAZIR IS DEAD

He throws the WAZIR's *foot into the pool with a splash, hurls his cloak over the torches, and races out. General pandemonium breaks out in the darkness as the guards and guests fish the* WAZIR's *body from the pool, and carry it out.*

OMAR's VOICE. Light the torches ! Light the torches !

Guards do so and lights come back up. The guests are clustered together, abuzz with excitement. OMAR *holds up his hand for silence :*

OMAR. Nobles of Baghdad, apparently our Wazir of Police was a
very poor judge of magicians. He has paid the ultimate price. [LALUME
enters. He bows to her as she passes him]. My dear lady, I commiserate.

LALUME [*Coolly*]. Not for my sake, I hope. [THE POET, *dishevelled but
unresisting, is dragged in. She hurries toward him, admonishing the guards*].
Don't harm him ! No sentence has been passed !

MARSINAH *is brought in.* THE POET *tries to go to her but the guards restrain him.*

THE POET. Marsinah !

MARSINAH. Father ! Father, what is it ? Why are they holding
you ?

LALUME [*To the guards*]. Release him !

They obey. THE POET *envelops* MARSINAH *in his arms.*

THE POET [*Soothingly*]. Listen to me, the Wazir will not harm you
again. He is dead.

MARSINAH [*Dazed*]. Is it true ? Am I free ?

LALUME [*Brightly*]. It's true, my dear. Our husband is dead.

MARSINAH *sobs in relief and buries her head on her father's shoulder. The* CALIPH *enters.*

THE POET [*Addressing the* CALIPH *over* MARSINAH'S *shoulder*]. **Noble Caliph, Highest of the High . . .**

CALIPH [*In a cold rage*]. **Silence! For a crime such as yours there is no defence to be spoken!**

THE POET. **No, All Highest, no defence to be spoken—but a living defence. A breathing one.**

> *He turns* MARSINAH *to face the* CALIPH. *The two lovers gaze at each other in disbelief and delight.*

CALIPH [*His eyes on* MARSINAH, *not moving*]. **Then—then the magician's story was true?**

MARSINAH [*Bewildered*]. **The gardener? Here?**

THE POET. **Not the gardener, my dearest Marsinah. The Caliph!**

> *She falls to her knees. The* CALIPH *tenderly lifts her to her feet.*

CALIPH. **Marsinah? Your name is Marsinah?**

MARSINAH [*Humbly*]. **Only Marsinah. I am no more than I seemed.**

CALIPH [*Softly*]. **And I am no *less* than I seemed—no less lonely, no less in love.**

> *He embraces her. As they stand clasped together,* LALUME *steps forward.*

LALUME. **All Highest, before you forget—will you pardon Hajj?**

THE POET. **No! Don't ask that! Under the circumstances, it would embarrass the All Highest to pardon his father-in-law!** [*To the* CALIPH]. **Oh, Prince of Justice, let me help you to compose this most difficult of verdicts against Hajj who, in his life, never once did right—and never once wronged anyone. Condemn the scoundrel to some dreadful—oasis . . . at least a week's camel journey away. Force him to take with him the widow of the late Wazir . . .** [*Aside to* LALUME *in a low voice*] **. . . and all the property she can get her hands on before the late Wazir's accounts are audited.** [*To the* CALIPH]. **Condemn him to lighten her sorrows, and to toil constantly to remove all grief from her heart.**

LALUME. **You have just sentenced yourself to a lifetime of hard labour!** [*She saunters out*].

MUSIC No. 42—FINALE ACT II

THE POET [*Continuing to the* CALIPH, *over music*]. **And finally, Oh, Prince of True Believers, take from Hajj his greatest treasure, his daughter Marsinah. Take her away forever—by marrying her to the end of her days.**

CALIPH [*Alight with love as he smiles down at* MARSINAH]. **Such is the Caliph's pleasure, and so he orders!**

THE POET [*Singing*]
> Play on the cymbal, the timbal, the lyre,
> Play with appropriate passion; fashion
> Songs of delight and delicious desire
> For the night of their nights!

CALIPH [*Singing*] **Come where the so well beloved is waiting . . .**

MARSINAH [*Singing*]
> **Where the rose and the jasmine mingle . . .**

CALIPH AND MARSINAH [*Singing together*]
> While I tell { him the moon is for mating
> { her the moon is for mating

CALIPH, MARSINAH, AND THE POET [*Singing together*]
> **And 'tis sin to be single!**

ALL [*Singing*]
> Let peacocks and monkeys in purple adornings
> Show her the way to my bridal chamber,
> Then get you gone till the morn of my mornings

After the night of my nights,
After the night of my nights!

Taking their cue from the song, the guests get themselves gone. The CALIPH *starts to lead* MARSINAH *out. She stops, begs her lover's forgiveness with a glance, and runs back to give her father a last hug of farewell.* THE POET *gazes after her fondly as she rejoins the* CALIPH.

CALIPH.   'Tis the night of my nights!

He departs with MARSINAH. THE POET *is now alone. He steps forward, faces the audience, and sings directly to them.*

THE POET [*Singing*]

Princes come, Princes go,
An hour of pomp and show they know;
Princes come,
And over the sands,
And over the sands of time
They go!

Seemingly in response to a gesture from THE POET, *ornamental screens on both sides of the stage begin to close in, as though an enormous book were being closed.*

Wise men come,
Ever promising
The riddle of life to know;
Wise men come,
Ah, but over the sands,
The silent sands of time,
They go!

The book has almost closed behind him. Now the house curtain begins to descend slowly.

Lovers come, lovers go,
And all that there is to know
Lovers know,
Only lovers know!
    [*He bows and the*

CURTAIN IS DOWN

PROPERTY PLOT
ACT I

SCENE 1. THE MOSQUE

On Stage: Faggot broom (Doorman of Mosque), stuffed burlap (set dressing), rug covering for step of Mosque, 3 chests, cover for chests.
Off Stage Right: Megaphone (Muezzin), coins (Merchants).
Off Stage Left: Crutch (1st beggar), hook arm (2nd beggar), 2 megaphones (Muezzin), coins (Merchants), wooden pail with garbage (Doorman), 2 swords (Bandits).
Personal Props: Dagger (Hassam Ben), parchment and pen (Marsinah).

SCENE 2. JAWAN'S TENT

On Stage: 3 chests (as Scene 1).
Off Stage Right: None.
Off Stage Left: Truss pole, bag of money (Jawan), small whip (Jawan), large whip (Bandit).

SCENE 3. BAZAAR OF THE CARAVANS

On Stage: 2 boxes, 1 large wicker basket, tambourine, RED veil, 2 veils (in wicker basket), large piece of coloured material, assorted silks (Dressing Booth Right), 2 small veils (Booth Left), assorted bird cages (Dressing Booth Left).
Off Stage Right: 3 bull whips (Wazir Police), brass cart (Merchant), Lalume's litter, Ababus's litter with silk cover, 3 shields (Ababus's), 3 swords (Ababus's), string of pearls (Pearl Merchant), 4 assorted wicker baskets (Merchant), basket of flowers (Flower Girl).
Off Stage Left: 2 oranges (Marsinah), bangle tree (Bangleman), 1 large carpet (Merchant), 1 small carpet (Rug Merchant), tray of silks (Silk Merchant), basket of fruit (Fruit Girl), basket of candy (Sweets Girl), tray of veils (Veil Merchant), basket of pastry (Baker), tray of spices (Spice Girl), chains (Slave Girls).
Personal Props: Bag of money (Hajj), pouches and coins (Merchant), swagger stick (Wazir), jug on strap (Omar).

SCENE 4. SIDE STREET

On Stage: None.
Off Stage Right: Chain and shackles (Wazir Police), dice and dice box (Wazir Police).
Off Stage Left: Hajj's litter with cushions, hookah, atomizer, lyre (Slave Girl), rope (Policeman for Slave Girls).

SCENE 5. GARDEN

On Stage: Bench and mound.
Off Stage Right: None.
Off Stage Left: None.

SCENE 6. A STREET

On Stage: None.
Off Stage Right: Caliph's litter, drum (Herald), spice tray (Spice Girl).
Off Stage Left: 3 snake boxes, veil, rug, 2 large carpet bags, 1 piece parchment paper, tray of veils (Merchant), basket of fruit (Fruit Girl), 2 large bundles of packages.

SCENE 7. WAZIR'S PALACE

On Stage: Throne—large cushion, 2 bolsters, 3 large cushions.
Off Stage Right: 2 seat cushions, handcuffs (Hajj), black table, 1 peacock fan, 3 swords (Guard), 1 scroll (Chief Police), parchment scroll (Wazir), Herald's staff, bag of money (Guard).
Off Stage Left: 3 large pillows, 1 peacock fan, 1 sword (Guard).
Personal Props: Amulet on chain (Wazir), Amulet on chain (Jawan).

ACT II

SCENE 1. WEDDING PROCESSION (Front of Traveller)

On Stage: None.
Off Stage Right: None.
Off Stage Left: 6 garlands (Dancers), wedding litter, 2 Herald's banners, 1 lyre, 2 lutes, 1 fly whisk, 1 Herald's staff, processional carpet.
Personal Props: 1 jug (Omar).

SCENE 2. GARDEN

On Stage: **Bench and mound.**
Off Stage Right: **Chest of jewels (Herald), Caliph's robe (Herald).**
Off Stage Left: **None.**
Personal Props: **Jug (Omar).**

> NOTE: All Wedding Procession Props in Act II, Scene 1, work again in this scene from STAGE RIGHT.

SCENE 3. PALACE ANTEROOM

NO PROPS

SCENE 4. WAZIR'S ROOFTOP PAVILION

On Stage: **2 benches with cushions (On Porch), couch with cushions and bolsters, 2 large pillows on side of couch, 2 small pillows on couch, streamer pole (attached to side of Porch).**
Off Stage Right: **Plume fan (Servant), tray with: bowl, spoon, 3 spice shakers, small fan.**
Off Stage Left: **Candy dish with rose, 3 roses, Emir crown (Wazir).**

SCENE 5. PALACE CORRIDOR (Front of Traveller)

On Stage: **None.**
Off Stage Right: **None.**
Off Stage Left: **Pedestal, ornate hand mirror.**
Personal Props: **Emir crown (Hajj), Jug (Omar).**

SCENE 6. ANTEROOM OF WAZIR'S HAREM

On Stage: **None.**
Off Stage: **Hair brush (Ababus).**

SCENE 7. CALIPH'S THRONE ROOM

On Stage: **2 mattresses and cover (IN Pool), Caliph's throne (with cushion seat), Wazir's throne (with 7 assorted pillows).**
Off Stage Right: **2 lyres.**
Off Stage Left: **Carpet (Ayah), silk curtain, 3 spears (Ababus).**
Personal Props: **Dagger (Hajj), 2 plaques (Hajj).**

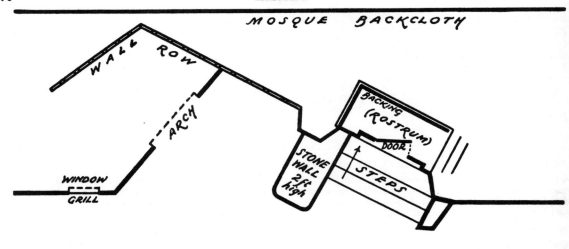

ACT I SCENE 1

ACT I SCENE 2

'BAZAAR' BACKING

(ROSTRUM)

ARCH   ARCH   ARCH

S T E P S

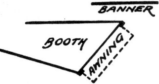
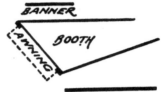

BANNER   BANNER

BANNER   BOOTH   AWNING

BOOTH   AWNING   BANNER

ACT I SCENE 3

'SIDE STREET' DROP

ACT I SCENE 4

'GARDEN' BACKCLOTH

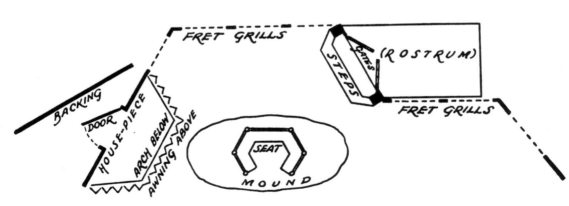

FRET GRILLS

(ROSTRUM)

STEPS   GATES

BACKING

DOOR

HOUSE-PIECE

ARCH BELOW

AWNING ABOVE

FRET GRILLS

SEAT

M O U N D

ACT I SCENE 5. ACT II SCENE 2

'CORRIDOR' GAUZE

ACT I SCENE 6

'THRONE ROOM' BACKING

WINDOW   GRILL FLAT   WINDOW

STEPS

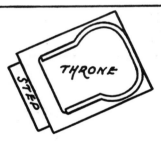

THRONE

STEP

ACT I SCENE 7

*GARDEN SET
BEHIND*

GAUZE TRAVELLER

ACT II SCENE 1
& SCENE 5

*GAUZE
PANELS*

ACT II SCENE 3

'GARDEN' BACKCLOTH (as in Act I Sc. 5)

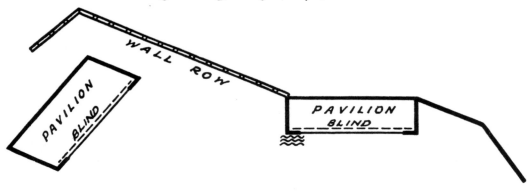

ACT II SCENE 4

CALIPH'S PALACE
SET BEHIND
PANELLED GAUZE

GAUZE PANELS

ACT II SCENE 6

'HAREM' BACKCLOTH

ROW OF ARCHES

(ROSTRUM)

ROW — OF — ARCHES

STEPS

ROW OF ARCHES

POOL

ACT II SCENE 7

21PB
6658

Printed by Loader Jackson Printers Limited